Advanced Praise for
Queer & Trans Advocacy in the Community College

"Read. This. Book! Our community college LGBTQ+ students are crying out for support and understanding. They want to thrive and succeed at our colleges and we need to develop our capacity to listen, learn, and engage with this critical student population."

—**Dr. Lori M. Berquam**, interim president, Mesa Community College

"As president-elect for the Association of California Community College Administrators (ACCCA), I see the value *Queer & Trans Advocacy in the Community College* adds to our call for equity and justice. This is an effective and practical tool for anyone who wants to understand how to be an advocate, accomplice, and ally to our LGBTQ+ family. Written with freshness, honesty, intensity, and power."

—**Wyman M. Fong,** president, Association of California Community College Administrators (ACCCA); national board member, Asian Pacific Americans in Higher Education (APAHE); vice chancellor of human resources for the Chabot-Las Positas Community College District

"I am thrilled to see new research on LGBTQ+ needs on community colleges. The number of LGBTQ+ centers on university campuses have grown over the last 20 years but most colleges do not have LGBTQ+ centers. This book expands the knowledge, dialogue, and efforts in LGBTQ+ services for students at community colleges. It is an exciting new resource for community colleges."

—**Bruce E. Smail**, director, LGBTQ+ Culture Center, Indiana University–Bloomington,

"*Queer & Trans Advocacy in the Community College* is good old fashion truth telling. An honest critique of the barriers systems impose on people and in particular those from the LGBT+ communities. The call to action is palpable and the guidance actionable. Community colleges must welcome the challenge and aggressively respond to the pervasive needs of the queer and trans communities."

—**Melanie Dixon**, president of American River College, Los Rios Community College District

"*Queer & Trans Advocacy in the Community College* is a ground-breaking book. It offers valuable insights into the challenges that LGBTQ+ community college students face, and it provides concrete suggestions for how colleges can help this vulnerable population achieve their academic and career goals. This should be a must read for every community college professional who is dedicated to improving the diversity, equity, and inclusion climate at their college."

—**Erika Endrijonas**, PhD, superintendent/president, Pasadena City College/ co-chair, LGBTQ+ Presidents In Higher Education

Queer & Trans Advocacy in the Community College

A volume in
Contemporary Perspectives on LGBTQ Advocacy in Societies
Joshua Moon Johnson and Lemuel W. Watson, *Series Editors*

Contemporary Perspectives on LGBTQ Advocacy in Societies

Joshua Moon Johnson and Lemuel W. Watson, *Series Editors*

Unheard Voices: A Collection of Narratives by Black, Gay & Bisexual Men (2021)
 Richard Greggory Johnson III, Kevin O. Spencer, and Annie Allen

Teaching the Teachers: LGBTQ Issues in Teacher Education (2020)
 Cathy A. R. Brant and Lara Willox

Queer People of Color in Higher Education (2017)
 Joshua Moon Johnson and Gabriel Javier

Queer & Trans Advocacy in the Community College

Joshua Moon Johnson
American River College

Emilie Mitchell
Cosumnes River College

Lemuel W. Watson
Kinsey Institute, Indiana University

INFORMATION AGE PUBLISHING, INC.
Charlotte, NC • www.infoagepub.com

Library of Congress Cataloging-in-Publication Data

A CIP record for this book is available from the Library of Congress
http://www.loc.gov

ISBN: 978-1-64802-920-2 (Paperback)
978-1-64802-921-9 (Hardcover)
978-1-64802-922-6 (E-Book)

Copyright © 2022 Information Age Publishing Inc.

All rights reserved. No part of this publication may be reproduced, stored in a retrieval system, or transmitted, in any form or by any means, electronic, mechanical, photocopying, microfilming, recording or otherwise, without written permission from the publisher.

Printed in the United States of America

*To all the young and old who have struggled with their identities—
to know you are enough and are worth loving.*

Contents

Foreword xi
Acknowledgment xiii

1 **An Introduction to Queer and Trans Advocacy in the Community College** 1
    Overview of the Book 4
    About the Authors 5
    Shared Meaning of Terms 12
    Conclusion 16

2 **Historical Context and Perspectives for LGBTQ+ Centers/ Services** 17
    Establishment of LGBTQ+ Centers on University Campuses 21
    Establishment of LGBTQ+ Centers on Community College Campuses 22
    Conclusion 27

3 **Identities, Intersections, and Student Support** 29
    Queer and Trans Students of Color 30
    Current and Former Forster Youth 31
    Abuse, Neglect, Family Rejection, and Entry Into Foster Care 32
    Educational Attainment by Current and Former Foster Youth 33
    Carceral System-Impacted Students 35

Issues Faced by Carceral System-Impacted Queer
and Trans Students 37
Tips for Serving Queer and Trans System-Impacted Students 38
Homelessness, Food Insecurity, and Economic Disadvantage 39
Issues Faced on Community College Campuses for Housing
Insecure, Food Insecure, and Economically Disadvantaged
Queer and Trans Students 42
Tips for Serving Homeless, Food Insecure, and Economically
Disadvantaged Queer and Trans Students 42
Age, Work, Parenting, and Geographical Limitations 43
Conclusion 45

4 Institutionalizing LGBTQ Efforts 47
Creating Missions, Vision, and Program Goals 49
Audiences and Services 49
Involving the Stakeholder 53
Getting Data 54
Staffing and Hiring 56
Common Staffing Models at Community Colleges 56
Hiring Considerations 58
Budgets and Funding 59
Space and Centers 59
Policies and Protocols 60
Communication and Outreach 61
Understanding Socio-Political Climates 62
Challenges 63
Conclusion and Successes 65

5 Building Partnerships for Impact 67

6 Practitioners' Voices 75
Introduction 75
De Colores: Sense of Belonging for QTPOC Community
College Students: A Practitioner's Perspective
by Dr. Angel Gonzalez 76
Supporting Community College Students at the
Intersections: A Practitioner's Perspective
by Dr. Raja Gopal Bhattar 83

Supporting LGBTQ+ Employees in the Community
College: A Practitioner's Perspective
by Dr. Claudia Mercado 87

7 Students' Voices 91

Considering a Student Voice: "You Know What They Say
About College"
by Elaine Nicholson 92

Considering a Student Voice: "Fronterizo"
by Cesar Vizcaino 94

Considering a Student Voice: "Restoring Our Communities"
by Alejandra Landin 96

Considering a Student Voice: "Doing Better: Holding Colleges
Accountable"
by Cadence Dobias 97

Considering a Student Voice. *My Closet's Embellishments*
by Ash Tandoc 100

8 Conclusion 103

Identity and Tokenization as an LGBTQ+ Professional............ 103
Finding Resilience 105
National Resources 108
Further Research and Practice 109

References 111

About the Authors 119

Foreword

When I was young, I scoured my school libraries to find a reflection of myself as a lesbian, though that wasn't a word I knew. In high school, in 1962, I finally found an entry in an encyclopedia to give more description. I believe it said something similar to a homosexual was a man who had sex with other men. Then when I looked up the word "lesbian," it said this was a woman from the island of Lesbos. I was lost... and what did the Isle of Lesbos have to do with me anyway???

Many years later, in 1994, I was hired to expand a small operation into an actual lesbian and gay student affairs office at the University of Michigan. With the incredible support of the Michigan administration, the concept of an LGBT center (I added the "B" and the "T." The "Q" came years later) caught on, establishing services for LGBT students and encouraging research about their lives. And in 1995 at Michigan, I founded Lavender Graduation to honor our LGBT students as leaders and scholars and to let them know they mattered to the academy. Yet, while LGBTQ+ work was beginning in Student Affairs back in the 1990s, LGBTQ history was still a well-kept secret.

I began work as the UCLA LGBT Center director in 1997 and oversaw the construction of the new center in 2003. I included a 400 square foot library in the new center so that students would have a place to find reflections of themselves and to learn their histories. Students could finally find accurate representations of who they are and from where they came! LGBTQ+ people of every race and nationality and culture came before us, paving the way for our freedom though they likely weren't aware of that. And Student Affairs came full circle: supporting research, offering services, and providing the reflections of our lives.

Research about and services for LGBTQ+ students began at least 2 decades ago. In 1998, the first book on LGBT campus work (Sanlo, 1998) was published. It helped people think about the importance of LGBT work for student health and persistence to graduation. It also helped faculty and administrators understand that not all LGBT people are White; our campus communities are as diverse as this country itself. But the work seemed to slip by community colleges. Today, after many advances in LGBTQ+ work in higher education, especially in Student Affairs, community colleges seem to be the last frontier.

In my 2004 article in the *Journal for College Student Retention*, I called for research to examine the lives of lesbian and gay students longitudinally. That article was revisited in 2012 (Sanlo, 2012) in the *Community College Journal of Research and Practice* to focus specifically on community colleges.

Queer and Trans Advocacy in the Community College moves beyond the early work. Drs. Emilie Mitchell, Joshua Moon Johnson, and Lemuel W. Watson take community college LGBTQ+ issues out of the academic closet and place them, finally, in practical light. They reflect the need and offer the skills for LGBTQ+ work on your campus. And yes, it also presents LGBTQ+ history so that our lives are finally reflected in Student Affairs literature.

This book is an important and necessary tool for community college administrators, faculty, and staff. Our students—our heroes and sheroes and they-roes—need you to be an informed ally. I have no doubt you'll find what you need in these pages.

—**Ronni Sanlo, EdD** (she/her/hers)
UCLA LGBT Center Director Emeritus

Acknowledgment

We first want to thank those who contributed to make this book happen. The student voices were powerful contributions; thank you Cesar, Alejandra, Ash, Cadence, and Elaine. We are also grateful to our contributing authors: Raja, Claudia, and Angel.

(Emilie) Thank you to my amazing colleagues who fight every day for our students, to my family for supporting me and reminding me that tomorrow the sun will rise again, and to my co-authors for writing this book with me.

(Joshua) I am thankful to all the LGBTQ+ students who never gave up, made a way when no educator supported them, and pushed to leave their colleges in better places for the generations who would come after them. I am thankful to those students who made sacrifices and took risks because they knew they deserved better and their fellow LGBTQ+ students also deserved better. I am thankful to those educators who might have been the only ones at a college who were vocal and advocated for LGBTQ+ students, who opened their office doors when no one else saw our LGBTQ+ students, and who offered food and love to those who were abandoned by their families. Our colleges and our society only get better when we take risks, share love, and hold our institutions accountable. The risks taken and the love shared has literally saved the lives of our LGBTQ+ students. I thank you.

(Lemuel) I am forever grateful for the life I have been given to live. I have lived long enough to know that everything I have experienced leads me to be able to love the man in the mirror that is looking back. It is with a multitude of love and thankfulness for which I have for the individuals who have imparted wisdom to me, given me strength to accept myself as I am, and the courage to show up without apologies. I am grateful to continue to work with such wonderful colleagues as co-authors. My co-authors continue to give me wisdom and courage to be curious in ways that helped me to become more of myself. Their energy and hope in what the world can be has been inspiring.

1

An Introduction to Queer and Trans Advocacy in the Community College

> *I used to think I was the strangest person in the world but then I thought there are so many people in the world, there must be someone just like me who feels bizarre and flawed in the same ways I do. I would imagine her and imagine that she must be out there thinking of me, too. Well, I hope that if you are out there and read this and know that, yes, it's true I'm here, and I'm just as strange as you.*
>
> —Frida Kahlo

> *If I wait for someone else to validate my existence, it will mean that I'm shortchanging myself.*
>
> —Zanele Muholi

During the first part of the new century, there has been significant research focusing on how LGBTQ+ students experience higher education (Ellis, 2009; Johnson, 2012; Leider, 2012; Nicolazzo, 2017; Renn, 2010; Robinson, 2019; Sanlo, 2004; Sanlo et al., 2002; Watson & Johnson, 2013; Wimberly, 2015). Renn (2010) explains, "Higher education research related to LGBT/queer people has evolved in tandem with activism movements, following trends seen in research on more readily identifiable populations of underrepresented campus groups" (p. 133). However, lesbian, gay, bisexual, transgender, queer, and other marginalized sexual orientations and gender identities (LGBTQ+) continue to face marginalization, mistreatment, violence, and disproportionate impacts within higher education and specifically in community colleges.

LGBTQ+ issues continue to evolve and warrant study and understanding for practice and for research. There is much need for specific literature to guide community colleges as they aim to serve diverse and marginalized students—many of whom are LGBTQ+. Even as LGBTQ+ literature has become much more prevalent in the last few decades, there is still far to go. In addition, there is such diversity within the LGBTQ+ community with terms and identities being fluid and dynamic. However, Renn (2010) shares that "queer is used by many LGBT people as an identity category including sexualities and gender identities that are outside heterosexual and binary gender categories" (p. 132).

The majority of the literature on LGBTQ students takes place in the 4-year institutional context and describes theoretical and developmental models developed using traditional-aged, racially homogeneous, 4-year college students" (Zamani-Gallaher & Choudhuri, 2011, pp. 47–48). Therefore, more understanding about policies, practices, and students' day-to-day experiences in educational organizations is needed, especially at the community colleges. Few if any research studies or articles address LGBTQ+ advocacy on community college campuses. There are more than 1,000 community colleges in the United States. Even with the extraordinary number of students that the community college system educates, only around 10 institutions nationally have paid staff to provide LGBTQ services to students. The Consortium of Higher Education LGBT Resource Professionals (n.d.) maintains a list of institutions with an office or center that has at least one 50% professional level employee whose job description names serving LGBTQ+ people as primary responsibility of the job.

Garvey, Taylor, and Rankin (2015) further confirmed this gap in the literature about the lack of research and information examining the experiencesof LGBTQ+ community college students compared to racial/ethnic minorities, students with disabilities, women, and first-generation students. In considering a deeper understanding of issues for LGBTQ+, we need to also be cognizant of the lack of methodological rigor that would involve intersectionality, campus climate, socio-emotional, socio-political, and socio-culture intersections of identity, and how they interaction with the campus climate and environment for LGBTQ+ community college students. We must be diligent in asking questions of relevancy for research and practices in considering the experiencesof students at community colleges (Zamani-Gallaher & Choudhuri, 2011). Given the fact that community colleges enroll nearly half of all undergraduate students in the nation—10 million students—a closer look at the experiences of students, specifically LGBTQ+ students, seems necessary (Bailey et al., 2015). LGBTQ+ advocacy should continue to be a priority in U.S. higher education, and it is time to bring this focus to community colleges.

Community colleges are beginning to put a more considerable emphasis on understanding and supporting this community. For example, The California Community College (CCC) system's 116 colleges now require all campuses to create a plan on how to improve success rates of LGBTQ+ students. The CCC is the largest higher education system in the country serving over 2 million students. This book will combine relevant research and guidance on practices to aid colleges in establishing services and programs to build effective LGBTQ+ services on their college campuses.

In this chapter, we will share an overview of the book and the three authors, Joshua, Lemuel, and Emilie, will each share narratives about experiences along our journey in life and leading up to this project. In addition, we share a plethora of vocabulary that will be useful to the reader for understanding the content and voices that are shared throughout the text.

This book was written as a practical tool for administrators, faculty, and staff in community colleges. Regardless of our readers' familiarity with LGBTQ+ literature and research, this book should provide new insight, research, narratives, and tools to serve those marginalized on college campuses and in communities. Because of the need, we also wrote this book as a tool for graduate programs that are related to the helping professions, but especially higher education, student affairs, and community college leadership. There are growing numbers of master's and doctoral programs focused on community college leadership and it is critical to include information and reflection on equity, justice, and liberation. This book will also be a powerful tool for those who attended community colleges, work in 4-year schools who have community college transfers coming, and for anyone who wants to better understand how to be an advocate, accomplice, and ally to the LGBTQ+ community.

There is much to continue to learn about our world and our many communities. No hierarchies need to be invoked to listen, learn, or engage in the understanding or each other which leads us to understanding ourselves. The world is changing at a very quick pace, and we must continue to grow our knowledge and improve practices. This book is written at a specific time, place, and context, and the knowledge we provide should be critiqued, questioned, and pushed to the next level. We build this work off of monumental LGBTQ+ rights leaders, civil rights leaders, critical race theorists, queer theorists, and feminist studies theorists.

Overview of the Book

This book includes a variety of formats, and a key focus is a practical "how-to" component to guide institutions as they aim to create LGBTQ+ services or centers. The term "centers" can often refer to a physical space where LGBTQ+ people know they belong and can exist in a safer space; however, some institutions use the term to refer to an office or program. There is still much foundational work that needs to be done, and the chapters provided include research from community colleges who have established LGBTQ+ services and knowledge that other colleges can use. Another section of this book includes an overview of the diversity of identities often present within community colleges. Community colleges have differences in operations from 4-year institutions; moreover, the students present at community colleges often represent some of the most marginalized populations in our society. Another component of this book is several sections featuring contributing experts who can offer insights, research, and perspectives based on their experiences in higher education. The final component of this book is powerful narratives of LGBTQ+ community college students. There were multiple community college students who shared powerful essays and creative work about their experiences at a community college.

In order to gain a broader understanding of what community colleges are doing to serve LGBTQ+ people at their colleges, we developed a survey and distributed it to community colleges that we could identify as having some efforts dedicated to LGBTQ+ students and others in their college communities. Throughout this book we will be utilizing findings from this survey. We utilized the Consortium of Higher Education LGBT Resource Professionals (n.d.) database to identify colleges across the country. The consortium lists institutions that have dedicated centers and at least one paid person working in the center. We expanded that list to several other colleges that contacted us and identified as having resources for LGBTQ+ people.

The survey was sent to 15 colleges across the United States and 10 colleges completed the survey. All of the colleges were public community colleges; most institutions were on the West Coast of the United States. The majority of colleges that replied are a part of the California Community College System. The colleges ranged in size from 8,000 students to more than 30,000 students. Half of the institutions were Hispanic Serving Institution (HIS) and/or Asian American and Native American Pacific Islander-Serving Institutions (AANAPISI). The colleges ranged in location from metropolitan city centers, to suburbs, rural, and small cities. There was no consistent theme in geographic city type. The survey was sent by email to staff identified in those centers during the Spring of 2020. This was also during the COVID-19 pandemic, which could have affected responsiveness and the perspective of those being surveyed.

We asked 16 questions to gauge a better understanding of center staffing and operations, services provided, audiences focused on, funding models, how they were established, challenges faced, and successes as an LGBTQ+ center. We will use excerpts from this survey throughout this book in order to provide specific examples of how Community College LGBTQ+ centers have created services, structures, and programs to support their students towards persistence, graduation, and identity development.

This book is unique and fills a void in the literature. The purpose is to equity community colleges to develop services, centers, staffing, policies, practices, and climates that empower and enable LGBTQ+ people to succeed at their colleges. Many community colleges want to serve LGBTQ+ people, but have limited knowledge and resources provided for them. This book will provide practical tools supported by relevant research so community colleges can confidently take action.

About the Authors

Each of us as authors have different perspectives and experiences although we all identify within the LGBTQ+ community. We have different perspectives on the major theme of this work and how each of us came to understand, embrace, and advocate for space to exist for trans and queer individuals. We have learned and continue to learn about the trans community but acknowledge that this has not been our lived experience. Our individual identities and our career paths have similarities and many differences. We know that our work is more powerful in the collective versus as individuals. In order for our readers to better understand our perspectives and work, we will share more about our identities, ways of knowing, and career experiences.

Emilie Mitchell (she/her/hers)

I am a White, cisgender, queer, gender conforming, educated professional woman. I start my story this way to acknowledge the many privileges I am afforded based on the identities that our White heteronormative society values (e.g., my race, socioeconomic standing, and gender conformity). I am a child of the 1970s and 1980s. I was born several years after the Stonewall uprisings and the burgeoning of the civil rights movement for queer and trans individuals. I was also raised in the era of the AIDS crisis which ravaged the gay community. I was born to a mother who was a feminist and raised in a state where a proposition was put to a vote that would bar employing openly gay public-school teachers and other workers (Briggs initiative). In sum, I was born and raised in a time of deep ambivalence toward members of the queer and trans community.

When I "came out" in college, family members undoubtedly based on their own fears and experiences, explained to me very clearly that I would be unlikely to have everything I wanted in life (children, acceptance, and success). I thought that these were simply cautions from well-meaning if misguided family members—then some of them stopped talking to me and I became a family member people only whispered about. Many years later when I decided to become a parent, the inequities foretold by my family showed up again. When I was in graduate school and 8 months pregnant with my first child (2003), the health insurance program for dependents was cancelled through my university. Owing to the laws at that time that governed whether employers had to cover "domestic partners," I was not eligible to receive insurance coverage from my "domestic partner's" employer. We were very fortunate that my partner was a lawyer, and we had the financial means, we thought, to purchase insurance on the open market. However, owing to laws that allowed insurers to deny people coverage for a pre-existing condition (of which pregnancy was categorized) no one would ensure me and my child. Even with all the privileged identities I held, society had decided that my health and well-being, and that of my child, were less valuable. My daughter was born uninsured and we entered the health care system for those who have less, alongside so many of my students.

Fast forward several more years, and the passage of Proposition 8 (2008; California Courts, 2022) reminded my family and me that in the eyes of society we mattered less. For those unfamiliar, this voter approved proposition amended the California Constitution to enshrine discrimination. It stated that the rights and privileges conferred by marriage would only apply to heterosexual couples. In practical terms, this meant for my family (now with two children) that I would not be entitled to the social security benefits of my partner should she die; that if we ever moved to another state, we could lose any rights and privileges afforded to us under the separate and never equal system of "domestic partnership"; and that the availability of health coverage and access to care would be decided by the ideology of employers. Again, I was reminded of my family's cautions.

As I have reflected on these experiences and on some of the wins the LGBTQ+ community has celebrated, I now see that perhaps what my family was trying to tell me was less about individual incidences of discrimination, marginalization, and exclusion that almost all queer and trans folks experience, but rather about the ways in which systems (laws, schools, and policy) seek to keep people from the full range of benefits a society offers. It is from this perspective that I come to this work. It is my pleasure to serve as the faculty coordinator for the American River College Pride Center and a psychology professor. I earned my PhD in social psychology from the University of California–Davis and have taught human sexuality for close to a decade. I have written and presented across the state on creating affirming and supportive community college campuses for queer and trans students. I am committed to dismantling the systems that exclude and marginalize queer and trans individuals and recognize that interlocking systems of oppression further marginalize our community members who are also people of color, undocumented, differently abled, and poor. My passion and my trade are education; I seek to help reinvent the experience of community college for our LGBTQ+ students so that they can explore, thrive, and excel. To hopefully ensure that they will never be told that they must choose between who they are and a fulfilling and successful life.

Joshua Moon Johnson (he/him/his)

My path to serving as an advocate for social justice and the LGBTQ+ communities comes from my personal experiences as a feminine, gender non-conforming, queer, multiracial, Asian American, White American, Christian, southern boy who is an amateur drag queen at times. I grew up in Mississippi and was raised by a Korean mother and White American father who were and are both Pentecostal evangelical ministers. My racial identity, Christian faith, sexual orientation, and gender expression, have deeply impacted all aspects of my journey including my educational path and career choices and experiences.

I currently serve as a dean of Student Services and Title IX coordinator at American River College (community college) in Sacramento. Much of my work outside of educational administration focuses on LGBTQ+ and intersectional work. I have published three other books; the first book, *Beyond Surviving: From Religious Oppression to Queer Activism* (2012) was a #1 best seller on Amazon.com for gay and lesbian activism. My second book is a co-edited volume about LGBTQ+ leaders in higher education, *Authentic*

Leadership (2013), in collaboration with Lemuel Watson. My third book was *Queer People of Color in Higher Education* (2017), in collaboration with Gabriel Javier. I have also published numerous other book chapters and articles on topics related to diversity and social justice. I previously served as the assistant dean/director of the Multicultural Student Center at UW–Madison and as the director of the LGBT Center at the University of California–Santa Barbara. I have also served as a faculty member at the University of Wisconsin–Madison, Semester at Sea/University of Virginia, Concordia University–Portland, and Binghamton University–State University of New York. I am a former chair of the NASPA (Student Affairs in Higher Education) MultiRacial Knowledge Community and held several positions with the Asian Pacific Islander Knowledge Community. I am honored to serve as the vice president of the board at the Sacramento LGBT Community Center and on the board and as the equity committee lead for the Association of California Community College Administrators (ACCCA).

I am the youngest of five children, and my four older siblings all attended community college. My educational path began at a 4-year university, but I attended a community college in Mississippi for two semesters while also being a student at the University of South Alabama. I received a doctorate in higher education and LGBT studies from Northern Illinois University, and a master's degree in student affairs and diversity from Binghamton University–State University of New York. I also have a master's degree in marketing analysis from the University of Alabama and a bachelor's in business (marketing) from the University of South Alabama.

I attended five different higher education institutions, and only one of them had a formal LGBTQ+ center or services. My educational experience was very rewarding and supportive in many ways; however, I often felt shamed, terrified, self-hating, and excluded because of my sexual orientation and gender identity. At almost every college I have been part of I have experienced hate crimes and/or biased incidents, and at times those were violent. When I faced this violence and hatred on a college campus, I had no one to tell and had no idea how to report or if I should report. I found ways to succeed in higher education, but my story is not normal. I also showed up as a student with other privileges; being male, being Christian, being able-bodied, having a White father, and even with my racial identity I was assumed to be a "good" student. Although I grew up in a working poor family, I still had access to health insurance and cannot remember a time when I did not have food or a secure place to live.

I approach this work with experience as an LGBTQ+ scholar and as having served as the interim director of the LGBT Center at Northern Illinois University, director of the LGBT Center at the University of

California–Santa Barbara, and as the dean of Student Services, Equity Programs, and Pathways at American River College, where I was able to establish the Pride Center in collaboration with Emilie Mitchell. As Emilie and I began creating LGBTQ+ services at a community college, we realized how little resources there were available to us, and we began documenting our process to establish an LGBTQ+ center. Emilie and I have since presented multiple times about how community colleges can institutionalize LGBTQ+ services at their colleges. As a Title IX coordinator, I actively find ways to include LGBTQ+ issues within sex and gender-based violence prevention work. In my role as an educator, writer, speaker, board member, and consultant, I aim to empower our organizations to do better in creating LGBTQ+ inclusive climates. I am committed to ensuring that community colleges sufficiently support LGBTQ+ students, so they can succeed and proceed to dynamic careers and/or transfer to 4-year institutions.

Lemuel W. Watson

There are generational differences I have dealt with as a middle age gay professional man. I have seen the world change around me over 5 decades with LGBTQ+ populations slowly coming out of the shadows and corners of life. I have been fortunate to live how I wanted to live in this world with the consciousness of who I am, considering the limitations and oppression that one of my natural inclinations would deal with in our social context.

As a child of the 1960s and an adolescent of the 1970s, I have been influenced by numerous changes that have shaped our history and our country. Born in the early 1960s and coming of age during so many cultural and societal changes, I saw a world that was only limited by my imagination. My family offered me such a perspective for being myself. Although I participated in playing house and with dolls at times, I did not think of myself other than a boy, cisgender, which I was born. As a child growing up in the Carolinas, I never dwelled on the fact that I was different; other than when people told me. Most of the time that difference was certainly not stated in terms of being gay. Statements like, "He is too pretty to be a boy" or "He is so sensitive" or "He is sissified" were often shared. Yes, at school, there were a few name callings; yet I noticed that other kids experienced similar bullying. Yes, I recall that there have been those moments where an incident or experience awakened me to the full extent of how some people perceived me.

My family sustained me and protected me from the harsh realities of society long enough to develop a strong sense of self. My siblings and I knew we were loved and encouraged to be ourselves as long as it was respectable, and we honored God and the Divine. When it came to my family values, I knew I had to respect my parents and seek to obey God. However, within these confinements, I also found a space of safety. My extended family consisted of many people who loved me and gave me words of wisdom. It was also an integrated world of races, ideas, and cultures. What I learned from family, community, and school was to take risks. Don't always follow the rules when the rules seem idiotic and contradictory to human rights and needs. I learned to embrace myself and follow my spirit, not necessarily "religion," while accepting the consequences of my actions and convictions as an individual.

A Southern American, I learned enough about my family's struggles and their values as a people and community that I never had to wonder about my background as an individual. I spent time with my elders and learned their value system. My parents modeled for me what it looked like to keep your head up and your vision clear. They modeled for me that anything is possible, regardless of place, race, or gender. Who I was, what I could become, was not conceived in what many will want to paint as the "racist South"; this is not to say that the South, nor the United States is null of a racist system, but that my community chose to give their children a more equitable environment. For this, I am grateful to my community and family. What I could become was not embedded in the limitations of my social class, economic status, or race. I know I am blessed to have had parents and grandparents to create a world around me that sheltered me from many harms.

The context of where one is born and raised has a powerful influence on developmental factors, life perspectives, and how one becomes in the world. My identity is not a textbook model. There are certain situations where I might feel more strongly about race than about sexual orientation or gender. However, for me, always number one is that I place Jesus Christ first—the rest will fall into place because I believe I am on a journey, and I have no idea about what the future holds. Hence, my identity comes from my sense of where I am from and has clashed at times with where I am meant to travel. Reconciling my commitment and dedication of my spiritual love for Christ and the love and physical desire I found for my first partner was pure hell. In fact, I lived an entire semester in a haze and depression dealing with it. I was ashamed for the first time in my life before God because I had been sexually active with someone. I felt that I had not lived up to my spiritual commitment to love God. I felt that my partner was evil in leading me down such a path, but I loved him dearly. I was so broken that I could not even pray because I felt God was so disappointed in me. It wasn't until an advisor from Campus Crusade for Christ told me "that nothing would ever separate me from the love of God" that I snapped out of the funk and embraced the fact that I am loved and treasured by God. The tension between God and gay was a relationship I had to face in my becoming that was psychological and emotional once I left home for college. This experience created a deep commitment to help other LGBTQ individuals understand spirituality, queer issues, and identity. Simply stated that one can embrace both and reject the perceptions of others and their labels surrounding such issues.

As an individual who does not define himself by boxes or labels, I am always understanding of others' perceptions and backgrounds and how they show up in the world, specifically how they make meaning out of their surroundings and especially, how they interact with me. I find that as one moves around the world with multiple populations, I am clearer about who I am and what my values are without imposing them upon others. In fact, the more secure I become with myself, the easier it is for me to allow people to be themselves and have their unique values, whether I believe in them or not. I have the power to decide how I will respond to anyone or any situation. Knowing this as a Black, gay, southern, spiritual man is comforting and empowering. I don't follow the overarching narrative that is touted about how we should see the world if we are a certain race or gender. We each have the power to make a difference in our immediate surroundings whether it be demonstrating openly and loudly or powerfully and silently in being our vulnerable authentic self. My first and basic theory or philosophy is to be "myself"; to recognize and respect individual differences and to do unto others as I have them do unto me or to do unto others as they wish and have the same applied to me.

Therefore, I choose not to get caught up in yet another category or box to put myself, and hope that others will also respect my perspective of not offering a pronoun here. It should be a choice, not a mandate regardless of one's perspective. I find boxes and labels oppressive and restrictive as an individual. To be clear, I support my colleagues, friends, students, and family who want to use pronouns; however, if one wants to speak to me or call for my attention, Lemuel, my name, is sufficient. I was not afraid or discouraged from exploring or pushing the boundaries of gender prescribed roles, like I am not afraid to speak up when my perspective is different or against the tide. Yes, there are always consequences and prejudices, and I have felt a few growing up. I found the courage and resilience to press through clouds of looks and comments, knowing that I had to survive. The simple matter is, it takes guts to express myself and put a future at risk. As I open up and share myself with the world, I do believe it will affect my life in many ways. Examples of such challenges have been given by my co-authors, Emilie and Joshua, as evidence. Should it matter? It will matter; it will have an impact.

I have been an advocate for equality most of my life. I speak up for those who are treated unfairly and have used my voice, power, position, privilege, and presence to not be silent during important conversations in order to educate and to change policies related to systemic discrimination toward underrepresented populations. As a professor, dean, and university administrator, affirming who I am with my husband is also important in every space I occupy. Yes, it matters! Our presence as a mixed raced couple who is comfortable with who we are is a testament to our past colleagues and activist work and impact, but also to our courage, hope, and faith in the future. Our stories are necessary because they continue to give the next generation of LGBTQ+ individuals examples, models, and the ability to dream in the possibilities for their lives.

Shared Meaning of Terms

It is important to understand that language and terms are ever evolving and are only a reflection of the current state of understanding. The words used by a community are based on history, a desire to be seen and understood, and sometimes the reclamation of terms formerly used to oppress and marginalize. Acknowledging that not all LGBTQ+ community members use the same terms or adhere to the same meanings of each term, it can be helpful to give some general definitions to help orientate and familiarize our readers, we will share explanations of the language that will be used throughout the book. At times the terms may be used interchangeably. To address the larger community, we may use "LGBTQ+" or "queer and trans," and we acknowledge that although those may seem like board terms, they still can leave others feeling excluded and marginalized. This is not an exhaustive list. Language, words, and identity are ever evolving. This is our best effort at the time of writing.

- **LGBTQ+**—A commonly used acronym to describe members of the community. The plus sign is a recognition that the acronym falls short of including all the expressions of sex, sexual orientation, gender identity, and gender expression.
- **Queer**—The term queer has a long and painful history for many gender and sexual minorities. For years, the term queer was used to denigrate and harass individuals and is illustrated in the common playground game of the 1970s and 1980s "smear the queer." As with many terms of oppression and marginalization, the term queer has been reclaimed by the community to be an omni-

bus term describing individuals with a non-normative identity (i.e., not straight and/or not cisgender)

Queer and Trans—It has been increasingly common to also see the community referred to as the queer and trans community. In this context these omnibus terms indicate that the community consists of two distinct and separate identities—sexual orientation and gender identity. Within each of these overarching identities there exists much variation. These broad terms allow for the ever-evolving terms associated with sexual orientation and gender identity.

Sex versus Gender—Unfortunately, all too often sex and gender are conflated in popular discourse. It is important to understand that ones' biological sex, or sex assigned at birth, is a wholly separate concept from ones' gender and gender identity.

Sex assigned at birth—The label you are assigned at birth based on the genitals and chromosomes you have. Individuals are generally assigned either "male" or "female." It is important to understand that even within the realm of biological sex, important variations exist.

Transexual—A less commonly used term which generally indicates an individual who does not identify with their sex assigned at birth and who has participated in medical interventions to have their physical bodies align with their gender identity. Medical interventions may include hormone therapies or surgical alterations of genitals. The term "transsexual" can feel hurtful to many and has been used negatively to label people.

Intersex—An umbrella term for individuals whose genitals, gonads, and/or chromosomes do not fit the typical definitions of "male" or "female."

Gender—Socially constructed ideas about behavior, actions, and roles a particular sex performs.

Gender Identity—Gender identity is one's' personal sense of their own gender. This is a spectrum not defined by discrete boxes and for many individuals may change over the course of their life as ones' understanding themselves evolves. Below are some common terms used to describe gender identity.

- **Transgender**—An adjective to describe an individual whose gender identity and/or gender expression differs from their sex assigned at birth. This is an umbrella term that encompasses any number of ways in which an individual's personal sense of their gender may differ than their assignment at birth.
- **Non-binary**—Someone whose gender identity is not exclusively man or woman. In recent years, some states have moved to recognize non-binary as additional gender option on legal documents (e.g., driver's licenses).

- **Cisgender**—An adjective describing someone whose gender identity is in accordance with their sex assigned at birth.
- **Gender Expression**—A term used to describe how one expresses their gender identity through outwardly observable characteristics such as behavior, dress, and mannerisms. Gender expression is a spectrum with feminine and masculine at the polar ends and androgynous as the center point.
- **Gender conforming**—Someone whose gender expression conforms to the norms of those who identify with a particular gender. For example, if an individual identifies as a cisgender man and wears a suit.
- **Gender non-conforming** (GNC)—Someone whose behavior or appearance does not conform to gender expectations. For example, if an individual identifies as a cisgender woman and wears a suit. It should be noted that what is characterized as non-conforming varies considerably across cultures and historically. For example, within the contemporary "American culture," gender conforming expectations are stronger and options for expression more limited, for those who identify as "man" than those who identify as "woman." It is also important to remember that GNC (gender non-conforming) is also a variation of gender identity.

Sexual Attraction—This is also sometimes referred to as physical attraction. In the broadest sense, sexual attraction is attraction that is based on sexual arousal or sexual desire.

Allosexual—An adjective that describes individuals who experience sexual desire for other individuals.

Demisexual—Individuals who experience sexual attraction only after an emotional connection occurs. Individuals who identify as demisexual may not experience arousal based solely on sexual desire.

Asexual—This term describes an individual who does not experience sexual or physical attractions. Importantly it should be stated that asexual individuals often desire and experience fulfilling romantic relationships that are absent the sexual desire or attraction.

Sexual Orientation—Sexual orientation is a term that broadly describes who an individual is sexually and/or romantically attracted to. It is important to state that sexual and romantic attraction are distinctive types of attraction and individuals may possess the desire for romantic relationships without sexual desire. The definitions below attempt to encompass this complexity of sexual orientation, but we

An Introduction to Queer and Trans Advocacy in the Community College ▪ 15

recognize that there exists far more variation in sexual and romantic attraction then are captured with definitions.
- **Bisexual**—A person who is sexually and romantically attracted to two genders.
- **Pansexual**—An individual who is sexually and romantically attracted to all genders, sexes, and gender identities. Said another way, pansexual individuals are attracted to the person irrespective of all aspects of sex and gender.
- **Lesbian**—A woman is attracted (sexually and romantically) to women.
- **Gay**—Although this term is used by both those who identify as men and women, it generally is understood to mean men who are attracted (sexually and romantically) to men.
- **Straight**—An individual who is attracted to the "opposite" sexed individuals.

Phobias—Although the term phobia is generally understood to mean an extreme and irrational fear of something, in terms of phobias related to the LGBTQ+ community the meaning is a bit different. As directed toward the LGBTQ+ community, phobias indicate fear, but it also relates to prejudice and a propensity to discriminate and mistreat members of the community.

Homophobia—A dislike or prejudice against people who are not straight.

Transphobia—A dislike or prejudice against people who are not cisgender.

Advocacy—Public support of LGBTQ+ and active action to address issues especially at a policy level.

Ally—Someone who is not in the LGBTQ+ community but strives to support and advocate for LGBTQ+ issues. One does not get to choose the "ally" term, but can strive to being an ally with specific actions.

Privilege—Unearned benefits in society because of one's identities. Nearly all people have specific social identity privileges that benefit them in daily interactions and systemic and institutionalized manifestations.

Cisnormativity—The assumed norm is that people are cisgender and the polices, practices, and cultures defer to cisgender people as the standard and norm.

Heteronormativity—The assumed norm is that people are heterosexual and the polices, practices, and cultures defer to heterosexual people as the standard and norm.

Sexual minority—Those who are not heterosexual.

Two-spirited—2-spirited people of the 1st Nations ("In the Beginning," n.d.) is an ancient concept where someone carried two spirits, which were male and female. These individuals were seen as a third gender and were often honored and revered.

Gender minority—Someone whose identity is other than cisgender.

Conclusion

This book is the beginning of a journey, and we hope that it shares new knowledge and invokes action. Community colleges vary in resources, knowledge, and political landscape; however, they all have queer and trans students and can do better in keeping them safe and helping them succeed in higher education and as humans in society. This book will not be able to capture every component needed to fully develop LGBTQ+ services at a community college, but it will lay a foundation and provide many issues and topics to consider. Community colleges cannot wait until they have it "all figured out" or wait to "solve racism" before considering other oppressed communities—especially as we think about the intersection of identities with race, gender, sexuality, and many other identities existing within our students' lives. The time is now to act; let's do this!

2

Historical Context and Perspectives for LGBTQ+ Centers/Services

> *I dare to dream of a world where people can dress, speak, and behave how they want, free from mockery, derision, judgment, harassment, and danger. This is what I want. Who's with me?*
>
> —Juno Dawson

In an effort to understand LGBTQ+ movements on college campuses, it is critical to have a broader understanding of LGBTQ+ oppression and activism in the United States. The queer history of the United States began before the inception of the nation. Indigenous populations for centuries accepted same-sex marriages and normalized non-binary gender categorizations (Gutiérrez, 1991; Hurtado, 1999). When the Spanish arrived to colonize the Americas, they immediately denounced the indigenous population's sexual and gender norms and offensively labeled biological males who expressed their gender in feminine ways and took on women's roles in their tribes, *berdache*, translated as a sodomized boy prostitute. Historian

Deborah Miranda (2010) describes Spanish colonizers genocidal policies against third-gender indigenous peoples as gendercide. European colonizers like the Spanish and the English understood gender transgression to be reducible to homosexuality and arrived in the Americas with the belief that same-sex relationships were a disruption to God's will of procreation and a desecration of human anatomy. As they established their economic and political power in the Americas, European colonizers murdered indigenous communities, stealing land, and indoctrinating the indigenous populations to believe that same-sex relationships and gender transgression were unacceptable forms of behavior (Bronski, 2011; Gutiérrez, 1991; Hurtado, 1999; Miranda, 2010). The colonization of the America's coincided with the establishment of higher education in the United States.

The U.S. society has defined what is appropriate for Christian behavior and given this dedication and devotion for those behavior, queerness, or an alternative way of being sexually meant public and personal suffering. The reason for this suffering is due to alternative lifestyle choices are perceived, by dogmatic fundamentalist Christians, as contrary to God's plan; and one was committed as mentally ill and suffered at the hands of others for healing or curing (Bronski 2011). Queer individuals also dealt with strict societal codes of behaviors and laws which they live in constant fear of accusations or risky behaviors to include cross-dressing, sodomy, or other acts of intimacy between same sex as illegal. Libraries are full with stories from history about the suffering of queer individuals and the harassment and punishment they faced, and the U.S. major cities were no exception. In fact, many of the laws that affected queer people were intended, according to historian Clare Sears (2015), to impose "moral order in municipalities in order to make them safe for 'good' white middle- and upper-class citizens by excluding gender [and sexual] 'outlaws' from public spaces. Predictably, the police targeted, in particular, queer people of color, immigrants, and low-income people for discipline and punishment" (Ritchie & Whitlock, 2018, p. 303).

Against all odds, queer people manage to create spaces and places to build communities. Harlem, New York, was one such neighborhood that welcome people of all individual expression to be themselves. Queer individuals created clubs, bars, speakeasies, and house parties to celebrate themselves and lifestyles. Writer, musicians, and creative individuals found a home to expressed themselves as gender non-conformists.

As stated in the Exploring Disproportionate Impact: LGBTQIA+ report by American River College (2021, p. 12), according to Stryker, 2017, "Transgender people, particularly trans people of color and poor trans people, often led resistance to this police harassment, even in the 1950s and early to mid-1960s, years before Stonewall. For example, in May of 1959 at Cooper's donuts in Los Angeles, a racially mixed crowd of trans and gay customers resisted the police when they arrived to arrest them. In San Francisco in 1966 when police arrived at Compton's cafeteria in the Tenderloin district to arbitrarily arrest the late-night crowd of drag queens, hustlers, and others, a riot broke out; ultimately, the riot combined with other forms of activism, resulted in long-lasting institutional change in San Francisco."

In addition, some homophile groups in the mid 19 century wanted to appear more cisgender and straight with the hopes of being accepted by straight society. The differences in ways of being in the queer community continue to be problematic for transgender people and non-cisgender presenting individuals. (Bronski 2011).

Transgender people, particularly trans people of color and poor trans people, often led resistance to this police harassment, even in the 1950s and early to mid-1960s—years before Stonewall. For example, in May of 1959 at Cooper Do-nuts in Los Angeles, a racially mixed crowd of trans and gay customers resisted the police when they arrived to arrest them. In San Francisco in 1966 when police arrived at Compton's Cafeteria in the Tenderloin district to arbitrarily arrest the late-night crowd of drag queens, hustlers, and others, a riot broke out; ultimately, the riot combined with other forms of activism, resulted in long-lasting institutional change in San Francisco (Stryker, 2017).

In the 1950s and 1960s, homophile groups' efforts to appear respectable to straight people involved mandating a dress code to send a message to straight society that gay people were just like them: men should dress in masculine attire and women should dress femininely—a policy that further marginalized transgender people and gender non-conformists. This lack of solidarity around the rights of transgender people would continue to plague gay and lesbian rights activism over the next several decades, which ultimately would lead transgender activists to strike out on their own to advocate for their rights and to bring about change in the mindset of the broader gay community today (Bronski 2011). Often, changes in society promote changes in our families and organizations and notions of rights and freedoms follow students into their higher education and post-secondary experiences.

With the increase in historical studies of Stonewall, the fact that gender-variant people, queers of color, and gay street kids were at the front lines has become more evident. However, the continued resistance to this narrative by assimilationist gays and the view of Stonewall as a disconnected, exceptional moment of gay revolt, has allowed only traces of the wider context of White supremacy, class oppression, transphobia, and hegemonic reformism to be brought to light. The resistance that Street Transvestite Action Revolutionaries (STAR) faced as a multi-racial group of revolutionary street queens illuminates the wider dynamics of the gay liberation movement and allows us to understand the foundation upon which the current White supremacist, cissexist, middle-class gay assimilationist movement is built upon (Riemer & Brown, 2019).

Sylvia Rivera and Marsha P. Johnson were not respectable queers, nor were they posterchildren for the modern image of "gay" or "transgender." They were poor, gender-variant women of color, street-based sex workers, with confrontational, revolutionary politics and, in contrast to the often abstract and traditionally political activists of Gay Activists Alliance, focused on the immediate concerns of the most oppressed gay populations. Within the predominantly White, non-gender-variant, middle-class, reformist gay liberation movement, Sylvia and Marsha were often marginalized, both for their racial, gender, and class statuses, and for their no-compromise attitudes toward the gay revolutionary struggle. Initially in public support of the Gay Rights Bill (Riemer & Brown, 2019), Rivera felt betrayed when the bill was passed to become New York law in 1986. She felt extremely disappointed because the bill excluded the rights of the transgender community.

Johnson first began wearing dresses at the age of five but stopped temporarily because she would get harassed by boys near her house. She described being the victim of sexual assault as an adolescent. Johnson's mother told her that being homosexual is like being "lower than a dog." Rivera was poor, trans, a drag queen, a person of color, a former sex worker, and someone who also experienced drug addiction, incarceration, and homelessness. For all of these reasons, both Johnson and Rivera fought for not only gay and trans rights but also racial, economic, and criminal justice issues (Brown, 2019).

Shortly after the 1992 pride parade, Johnson's body was discovered in the Hudson River. Police ruled the death a suicide, but friends and the local community insisted Johnson was not suicidal and noted that the back of Johnson's head had a massive wound. On February 19, 2002, Sylvia Rivera died from liver cancer at Saint Vincent's Catholic Medical Center in New York (The Legacy Project, n.d.).

As is true with changes in most organizations, but especially for public institutions, change is a combination of a groundswell of personal activism as well as supportive individuals in power, and often a history of discrimination and persecution. Activism and change in the public sphere impacts higher education climates and demands for change.

On college campuses prior to the late 1960s, many queer and trans students found ways to be themselves despite legal and social barriers, but usually did so in secret. College students rarely were open about their sexual or gender identities for fear of the legal consequences of violating the law, as well as fear that they would be disciplined or even expelled by their school's administration for being gay. In 1965, school officials forced openly bisexual student Stephen Donaldson out of his residential hall at Columbia University due to complaints by his roommates (Beemyn, 2003).

Students also formed organizations on college campuses starting in the 1960s, though before the rise of the politics of gay liberation, the groups tended to function in secret for fear of the repercussions. Likely, the very first officially chartered gay rights college student group was the Student Homophile League formed at Columbia University in April 1967, founded by a bisexual man. The formation of the group triggered a backlash after the *New York Times* ran a front-page article about it being granted a charter by the university, with the dean of the college saying it was "quite unnecessary" and the director of the counseling service claiming it would promote "deviant behavior" among students (Beemyn, 2003, p. 207). The university's administration allowed the group to keep its charter, despite this push back, but only under the conditions that it not serve a social function for fear it would violate New York State's anti-sodomy laws. The second-ever Student Homophile League was formed at Cornell University soon after. It faced similar challenges as the Columbia chapter—students who decided to become involved insisted on anonymity or using pseudonyms, fearing the consequences of visibility. Because so many gay, lesbian, and bisexual students tended to keep their identities secret it was quite difficult to recruit members; also, at first the meetings were not publicly advertised in order to safeguard the identities of current members (Beemyn, 2003). In its early years, the Cornell Student Homophile League attracted only a few women, and many of them were heterosexual allies. Also, the group was not inclusive of transgender students. Pauline Layton, a student who says they "felt stuck in a female body" was disappointed in the lack of awareness around trans issues by the gay students in the group, commenting, "Transgender and cross-dressing weren't much talked about circa 1968–1970" (Beemyn, 2003, p. 211).

Establishment of LGBTQ+ Centers on University Campuses

On the heels of the Stonewall Riots and emboldened by the quest for justice, activist such as Jim Toy founded the Detroit Gay Liberation Movement in 1970. Shortly thereafter, students at the University of Michigan (hereinafter UM) and local Ann Arbor community activities fought for the establishment of a chapter of the Gay Liberation Front (GLF) on campus. The GLF was formally recognized by the Student Government Council as a student organization in that same year. Despite an unsupportive college president, powerful allied administrators on campus combined with pressure from both the GLF and UM students ultimately led to establishment of the first staff office for queer students in September of 1971. Today that office is now called the Spectrum center and is a venereal office on the UM campus. To put this in some greater historical context, it was illegal in Michigan to participate in same-sex sexual activity until the Supreme Court Decision of *Lawrence v. Texas* in 2003.

Jim Toy, one of the founders of the Detroit Gay Liberation Movement and first director of the Spectrum center, is today 90 years old. We asked for an interview with him, but his current health struggles prevented him from answering our questions directly. That being said, the current Spectrum Director Will Sherry was kind enough to extrapolate from his many conversations with Jim. We think you will find his advice illuminating and empowering. The following narratives share insights into Jim Toy's role with early college LGBTQ+ advocacy.

1. How were you able to establish services for queer and trans students on the University of Michigan campus when the environment in the 1970s was decidedly hostile toward the LGBTQ+ community?
    Jim has often talked about an ally that worked within the campus administration that helped to advocate for the students and community cause. He has talked about the importance of this person's role with regard to having access and influence in important ways.
2. Can you describe some of the barriers you encountered as the center began?
    Jim talks about access to space and being denied the ability to convene a "gay" meeting in the Student Activities Building. He tells about how the group defied the institutional demand to not meet in the building and met there anyway. Then, the Student Activities Building was a student-run space and students had the keys.
3. What advice would you give individuals on campus who are trying to establish services on campus for queer and trans folks and facing resistance?
    Jim often tasks about persistence in this work. He always tells me to just keep pushing, keep making my voice heard, and continue to speak truth to power.

Establishment of LGBTQ+ Centers on Community College Campuses

The first community college to have a paid position to serve queer and trans students was the LGBTQ Student Resource Center on the Auraria campus in Denver, Colorado. The LGBTQ Student Resource Center is unique in that it serves the Community College of Denver, Metropolitan State University of Denver, and the University of Colorado Denver on one centralized campus. Astonishingly, this center was established in 1992 and began serving students at the Community College of Denver in 1994. To put this date in perspective, the next center or services office was not established until 2016 (Mt. San Antonio College)—some 22 years later.

Like so much of the fight for social justice, the establishment of services for queer and trans students was born of great injustice. The first LGBTQ+ center did face opposition. Following on the heels of attempts by the governor of Colorado (Ray Romer) and several cities (Aspen and Denver), opponents of justice and equity for the LGBTQ+ community mobilized voters and successfully amended the Colorado constitution blocked any municipality from providing protective status to queer individuals and become known as the Hate State in 1992. (*Romer v. Evans*, 1996). The passage of Amendment 2 in 1992 by nearly 54% of Colorado voters earned Colorado the dubious moniker of the "Hate State."

The story of securing funding to establish services to serve queer and trans students at the Community College of Denver follows the same pattern as the successful establishment of centers on nearly every campus. The beginning is student need and activism, in this case an undergraduate student at Metropolitan State University of Denver, Jody "Lucky" Andrade who established a student club. Working with other student and community groups focused on social and racial justice they successfully mobilized the student government (associated study body) to support the cause and leverage the funds that they control. They were also supported by a committed group of faculty and staff, Associate Vice President of Student Affairs Dr. Karen Thorpe, and Assistant Dean of Student Life Yolanda Ortega, Coordinator of Women's Services Tara Tul, and Associate Director of Student Activities Davidson Porter, who leveraged their positions and understanding of the college system to craft a proposal for funding a position to serve queer and trans students and push the idea up through the ranks of administration. The final element in this equation is a supportive college president. Ultimately, the college president at the time, Dr. Tom Brewer, approved the funding for the new position and the first center was thus established.

It is also worth noting that one of the California community colleges, the City College of San Francisco, has the first free-standing Department of LGBT Studies in the country. In Fall 1972, instructor Dan Allen from City College of San Francisco's English Department developed one of the first gay literature courses in the country. Due to illness, Allen turned leadership over to Dr. Jack Collins who continued to develop the curriculum at CCSF's gay and lesbian studies program from one course to four courses. A popular film class was well attended with over one hundred students at one point. The enrollment numbers and the support of a gay CCSF board member paved the way for the establishment in 1989 of the first Gay and Lesbian Studies Department in the United States. (The name was changed to Gay, Lesbian, and Bisexual Studies Department in 1996, and later changed to Lesbian, Gay, Bisexual, and Transgender Studies Department in 2006; https://www.ccsf.edu/academics/schools/social-sciences-behavioral-sciences-ethnic-studies-social-justice/lgbt-studies-department)

How LGBTQ+ Centers and Services Make a Difference

Like most missions of the LGBTQ+ centers at post-secondary institutions, the core mission remains focused on the support, education, and advocacy of the campus LGBTQ+ community, which includes students who are still negotiating their identity, and those who wish to remain invisible. Providing support involves a wide range of responsibilities to the students, institution, and community. Essentially, keeping students safe and well emotionally, mentally, spiritually, academically, and physically becomes a serious task given the vulnerability of LGBTQ+ students. For example, Rankin (2005) shares from a Campus Climate Report that "out of 1,669 LGBTQ+ students surveyed across the U.S., more than one-third experienced antigay harassment, 20 percent feared for their physical safety and 51 percent concealed their sexual orientation or gender identity to avoid intimidation" (p. 4). Rankin conducted a similar national study in 2010 and the results were similar.

There are clear results when an institution invests resources, people, curriculum, programs, and space to supporting LGBTQ+ students. In the absence of an LGBTQ+ center, Sanlo et al. (2002) conveyed that students' perceptions of the lack of support and not being seen were noted. The importance of various cultural centers has proven to be safe places for students and LGBTQ+ centers at colleges and universities have similar influences on the students experiences (Renn & Patton, 2010). LGBTQ+ centers can also provide a place for campus agents, community members, and students who are members of the LGBTQ community to interact for meaningful partnership, mentorship, and friendships (NSSE, 2020; Sanlo, 2004). Center, services, and staff are all critical to the success of queer and trans people in higher education.

Serving the Marginalized Within the Marginalized

LGBTQ+ advocacy has drastically improved in the last few decades, and higher education has come far with creating safer spaces. However, even within LGBTQ+ spaces, transgender community members are often pushed to the margins. The last few decades have focused on issues more relevant to cisgender gay and lesbian folks, such as marriage equality. Transgender youth are still invisible in most Western cultures because social structures assume a binary classification of gender. Individuals are expected to assume the gender of their biological sex as well as the gender expectations and roles associated with it. As nearly all people are classified as male or female at birth and gender norms are associated with that sex, those who express characteristics ordinarily attributed to the other sexes are stigmatized and seen often as social deviants. Inconsistency in the presentation between biological sex and gender expression is usually not tolerated by others (Gagne & Tewksbury, 1996). Because these individuals violate conventional gender expectations, they become targeted for discrimination and victimization. Thus, they become members of a marginalized and vulnerable population that experiences extreme psychosocial and health problems.

Many transgender individuals, however, seek services from identity-affirming service providers. As Ryan and Futterman (1997) indicate, and as these providers have come to learn, transgender people are generally more stigmatized than lesbians and gay people in contemporary society and require more support and services. For adolescents, this situation is even more difficult. Exhibiting gender-atypical behavior makes transgender youth an especially vulnerable population. Flaskerud (1999) describes vulnerable populations as "social groups who experience relatively more illness, premature death, and diminished quality of life than comparable groups" (p. xv). She relates vulnerability to a lack of resources and increased risk associated with discrimination, marginalization, and disenfranchisement. Facing significant prejudice and discrimination in schools, employment opportunities, housing, and access to health care, many transgender youth live outside mainstream society (Burgess, 1999; Mallon, 1999). As gender-atypical behavior is much less accepted in boys than girls, biological males who are transgender are most often the targets of verbal and physical abuse (Grossman & D'augelli, 2006). These social issues are mirrored in higher education.

However, current scholars and activist are speaking up and out during this time on our journey in history about many issues LGBTQ+ people face, especially transgender people. Z. Nicolazzo shared hir perspective of those professionals and students who are in higher education and are often asked to educate others about the specifics of LGBTQ+ individuals. Z shares an example of where a chief diversity officer was given a welcome where he thanked the queer students for helping to educate and teach others about various issues related to the LGBTQ+ individuals. Z goes on to say, "The CDO linked students' trans* and queer identities with a form of labor; namely, educating the heterosexual and cisgender campus population on issues related to gender and sexuality" (Nicolazzo, 2017, p. 107). Therefore, in essence one might assume that the CDO's notions were for trans and queer people to engage in the laboring of education and responding to community needs regarding diverse gender and sexuality unlike heterosexual and cisgender people who do not share equally in the burden. In fact, Nicolazzo (2017) goes on to elaborate that "the CDO suggestion that trans* people should teach others about gender was based on the commodification of diverse genders as something one could acquire through participating in a training, educational session, in-service, or class experience" (p. 108).

What if Marsha Johnson and Sylvia Rivera Were Your Students?

In reading about Johnson and Rivera, we must remember that we have students who are diverse in religion, generation, ethnically, racially, gender, and economically; and they will need to be served in our institutions. How do we best situate services and programs to address trauma, housing insecurity, and health in addition to the multitude of other issues that students bring with them to the college? Community college students continue to be engaged in multiple ways of advocating to survive and attempting to make their lives better through finding the appropriate individuals and resources to survive and succeed. How would your staff react to welcoming and encouraging Marsha or Sylvia in this moment? What would you need as an institution to be prepared? Who and what would Marsha and Sylvia see when they entered the Financial Aid office or when they attended student orientation? What questions will they be asked that will help them feel included? What processes will make them feel excluded, or force them to make a choice between their identities? How does the college participate in queer community events and take leadership on queer and trans advocacy in the community? How would Marsha and Sylvia know this? This chapter has shared the history of and context for LGBTQ+ centers and the challenges of the past and the future. Yet, LGBTQ+ centers continue to adapt and adopt with the changing times. What is important to remember is that there is no one size fits all or a single answer due to community colleges' location, sizes, community resources, and resources.

Therefore, as we continue to evaluate our work as LGBTQ+ individuals, we must strategically think about how to best position ourselves and resources within the institution for the greatest impact for our students, faculty, and staff. We must not allow ourselves and students to be used as objects of curiosity (Pusch, 2005) or commodities for various use by institutions. We are advocating that as educators we should all be supporting our community college students, especially LGBTQ+ students and other marginalized students. It is everyone's responsibility to serve them and guide them to the appropriate resources needed when there is not a center or designated individual to support LGBTQ+ students. Are our institutions and professionals living up to the greatest expectation of ethics if they are not prepared to serve and care for all students? This is the imperative for anyone who works in higher education in current times. It is the responsibility of the college leadership, faculty, and staff to advocate and support LGBTQ+ students' success and development.

Conclusion

Knowing our history is critical to the planning for the future. LGBTQ+ history in society is directly linked to the climate, policies, and practices in higher education. There is still little written about the history of LGBTQ+ issues and advocacy in the community college; however, we aim to use this book to ensure our future is deeply focused on making our colleges better for LGBTQ+ work. Even if little was done in community colleges in the past, we know we can make it better for our future students, faculty, and staff members. Society is continuing to push for more LGBTQ+ rights, and inclusion and community colleges should be a vital part of the next chapter.

3

Identities, Intersections, and Student Support

Remember this, whoever you are, however you are, you are equally valid, equally justified, and equally beautiful.
—Juno Dawson

Community colleges hold a very important role in our tiered system of higher education. These colleges pride themselves on being open access which enables them to provide an entry point into higher education for many students. According to recent research, 42% of all undergraduates are enrolled in a community college; this percentage translates into approximately 7.2 million students in the United States (Ma & Baum, 2016). Community college students often differ from those enrolled in traditional 4-year institutions. Community college students are more likely to be students of color, to be first in their family to have attended college, likely to be older when they start and finish their education, more likely to be a parent to a dependent child, and more likely to be more economically disadvantaged (Ma

& Baum, 2016). It is important to note that these identities and experiences are not mutually exclusive and can intersect and all reside within one queer or trans person's life. Little scholarship has been undertaken to understand the unique experiences, identities, and needs of queer and trans community college students. In the following sections, personal narratives of queer and trans student experiences will be shared, research will be presented on the unique needs of queer and trans (QT) community college students, and recommendations will be provided for developing services on community college campuses for queer and trans students.

Queer and Trans Students of Color

Whether we are talking about interactions with police, experiences in the classroom and on college campuses, or healthcare—race always matters! We do not now, nor have we ever lived in a "color-blind society." Black, indigenous, and all people of color experience a world that is fundamentally more hostile to them than White people. On community college campuses, over half of students enrolled are students of color (National Center for Education Statistics, 2021). Sadly, most community colleges do not survey their college students about sexual orientation or gender identity, thus, there are no means to determine what percent of community college students nationally are members of the LGBTQ+ community. There is an utter lack of scholarship on the experiences of Black, indigenous and other queer and trans people of color (BIQTPOC) on community college campuses. Research focused on BIQTPOC in 4-year college campuses found these students had more negative experiences than their White queer and trans counterparts (Rankin et al., 2010).

In order to understand the unique needs and experiences of QT students of color on our campuses, a theoretical framework is useful. One particular salient theoretical perspective is that of intersectional oppression developed by Dr. Kimberly Crenshaw (1989). We introduce intersectionality in this chapter and later expand upon it in Chapter 6, "Practitioners' Voices." At its most basic core, this framework helps us to understand that oppression is a system of layers, that each of us hold differing identities (e.g., sex, gender, sexual orientation, religion, ability, class, etc.), and that each of these identities may be privileged or oppressed within various systems (e.g., educational, employment, and legal systems). It further helps to illuminate the role of cumulative oppression. This is the idea that the more identities we hold that are oppressed, the more difficult in obtaining the benefits of a system. In the context of the conversation regarding serving on our campuses, it must be recognized that folks within this community

Identities, Intersections, and Student Support ▪ 31

not only face marginalization for their queer and/or trans identity, but also for their racial identity.

Issues Faced on Community College Campuses for BIQTPOC

1. Racism on campuses surfacing in violence, hostile climates, exclusion, and stereotypes
2. Lack of awareness of QT experiences in spaces focused on race
3. Racism and microaggressions in QT spaces

Tips for Serving BIQTPOC

1. *Address racism*—Address subtle and overt racism and discriminatory behavior in policies on the college campus as a whole, as well as in spaces devoted to serving QT students. Commit to the long-term journey of naming and addressing White supremacy.
2. *Representation*—Research indicates that students do better when they see themselves (e.g., their various identities) represented in their academic institution (Johnson, 2012). It is important to provide opportunities for students to see examples of thriving and successful QT faculty, classified professionals, and administrators of color. This should not be just one token person but should mirror the percentages of the student body. If the institution does not have this data, find ways to collect it.
3. *Integration across all aspects and programs of student services*—Ensure that QT perspectives are foundational in all aspects of student services. Conduct policy, practices, and campus climate audits.
4. *Inclusive policies and language*—Ensure that colleges have inclusive policies (e.g., bathrooms and building policies) as well as requiring the use of inclusive language across campus (e.g., name protocols and using gender neutral pronouns).

Thinking about systems, queer and trans individuals are more likely than their cisgender and heterosexual counterparts to be involved in two highly impactful institutional systems. Namely, these students are more likely to have been involved with the child welfare system and the incarceration system.

Current and Former Forster Youth

More community colleges have begun to create programs specifically serving former foster youth as they enter colleges, and there is an intersection of students who have been a foster youth and who are LGBTQ+ identified.

The Williams Institute at UCLA School of Law attempted to ascertain a population-based estimate of foster care involvement for LGBTQ (lesbian, gay, bisexual, transgender, or questioning) youth. This estimate was derived from the Los Angeles Foster Youth Survey (LAFYS) which randomly sampled close to 800 youths between the ages of 12–21 living in foster care. The results showed there were between 1.5 to 2 times as many LGBTQ youth living in foster care as LGBTQ youth estimated to be living outside of foster care with the majority of these young people being youth of color (Wilson et al., 2014). Additionally, while in the child welfare system, these same youth reported experiencing greater maltreatment at the hands of system providers. Specifically, almost 38% of youth in the foster care system reported poor treatment within the system connected to their gender expression, sexual minority status, or transgender status. Additionally, 7.5% reported having been kicked out of or run away from their foster or group homes for issues related to sexuality, gender identity, and gender expression (Wilson et al., 2014). In a recent study which focused on both LGBTQ (lesbian, gay, bisexual, transgender, or questioning) youth, foster care involvement as well as unstable housing researchers found that within the study sample over 30% of LGBTQ identified youths were in foster care and just over 25% were living in an unstable housing such as a friend's home, a motel, a shelter, or car (Baams et al., 2019).

Abuse, Neglect, Family Rejection, and Entry Into Foster Care

It is important to note that youth find themselves in foster or out of home placements because of abuse or neglect at the hands of parents or caregivers. In a meta-analysis comparing the rates of parental physical abuse and childhood sexual abuse for sexual minorities compared to those who reported being straight, researchers found that lesbian, gay, and bisexual adolescents were more likely to report both types of trauma. Specifically, compared with their heterosexual counterparts, those within the LGBTQ+ community were almost three times more likely to report childhood sexual abuse. In terms of prevalence, some 40% of bisexual females (40.4%), almost one-third of lesbian women (32.1%), and roughly a quarter of bisexual and gay men reported this form of trauma (24.5 and 21.2%, respectively). In terms of physical abuse, compared to heterosexual adolescents, those who were sexual minorities were 1.3 times more likely to report being physically abused by a parent or caregiver. The results clearly indicated that female and male bisexual adolescents were at particular risk for this form of trauma, 33.4% and 24.2%, respectively (Friedman et al., 2011). In addition to abuse, queer and trans individuals report experiencing a host of adverse childhood events including substance abuse by a parent, witnessing domestic violence, physical and sexual abuse, and having a parent incarcerated. Further, these experiences are also related to youth's level of gender conformity, with those youth whose gender expression was less in line with societal norms and expectations (gender non-conforming) experiencing more trauma (Baams, 2018).

Educational Attainment by Current and Former Foster Youth

Queer and trans individuals are more likely to have experienced abuse and adverse childhood experiences, more likely to be in some form of out-of-home care (group home or foster care), and more likely to have negative experiences in their out-of-home placements. Given the adverse life experiences detailed above, combined with a lack of a caregiver to help individuals navigate their educational experience, it is not shocking that educational attainment by former foster youth is lower than their peers. Specifically, foster youth are less likely to graduate from high school, less likely to attend college if they did graduate from high school, and less likely to complete their college degree if they attend college (Emerson & Bassett, 2008).

Issues Faced on Community College Campuses for Queer and Trans Current and Former Foster Youth

As community colleges are open access and many community colleges have support programs for foster youth or former foster youth, we see many foster youth attending community college. Although community colleges provide supportive programs, there are still a variety of challenges these students face, some include:

1. *Lack of family supports*—Queer and trans students who have been in the child welfare system often lack family supports. This lack of support translates into both a lack of emotional support to help weather the storms that inevitably come with new endeavors but also without assistance in navigating educational systems.
2. *Inconsistent educational history*—As noted above, education attainment by current and former foster youth are substantially lower than their counterparts with no child welfare involvement. Often foster youth's educational experiences are disrupted, changing schools often, repeated starts and stops to their education, and in-

ability to have educational challenges met by school staff because of frequent foster home changes.
3. *Basic Needs*—As students age out of the foster care system (varies based on state), these students are very likely to struggle with meeting their basic needs (e.g., housing, food, and transportation).

Tips for Serving Queer and Trans Current and Former Foster Youth

1. *Educational coaches*—One national program that has shown great promise in serving students who have been involved in the child welfare system is the Great Expectations Program in the Virginia Community College System. Utilizing the Casey Family Programs best practice model (Emerson & Bassett, 2008), this system has demonstrated improvements in the educational outcomes for current and former foster youth; including increased persistence and higher graduation rates ("Great Expectations: Fostering Powerful Change," n.d.). A hallmark of this program is a "coach." The coach is a caring adult on each campus who connects with the young person and helps provide navigation of college processes (i.e., how to apply for financial aid or how to enroll in classes), referral to important resources (i.e., housing and food resources), and most importantly, much needed consistent social and emotional support. The coaches should receive substantial training on identity development, specific to sexual and gender identity.
2. *Cultural competency and humility*—It is imperative that campuses provide services to the current and former foster youth that also affirms their sexual orientation and gender identity. A clear and concerted effort must be undertaken to acknowledge and honor the important ways in which sexual orientation and gender identity have influenced students' experiences in the foster care system, otherwise you risk alienating individuals—making them less likely to seek out these support services, or worse, inflicting more trauma on an already traumatized group of individuals. Programs must acknowledge and affirm the disproportionate involvement and aversive experiences of queer and trans young people in the foster care system, and competently help these young people navigate college and the world. For example, ensuring that the housing resources that are provided do not discriminate against queer and trans individuals and understanding how to help a student navigate the myriad of paperwork on a college campus if a student transitions in their gender identity. Examine policies, practices, and forms from an LGBTQ+ lens. There should be active collaboration

with college specific LGBTQ+ services and/or local LGBTQ community services.
3. *Trauma informed care and student services*—As noted above, queer and trans individuals are more likely to have histories of abuse and are more likely to end up in foster care because of parental neglect and abuse—experiencing more adverse experiences while in the foster care system. It is vitally important that programs on community college campuses that serve current and former foster youth are trained in trauma-informed care and student services.
4. *Scaffolded student services*—Students with a history of foster care involvement are likely to need help not only with how to navigate the systems of the college but also accessing tutoring services and important basic-needs assistance on campus and in the community. It is important that those individuals who are tasked with serving queer and trans current and former foster youth are capable of providing scaffolded student services that reach all of these needs.

Carceral System-Impacted Students

In addition to being more involved in the foster care system, queer and trans students are overrepresented in both the juvenile and adult incarceration system. Community colleges are also beginning to focus on supporting students who are currently experiencing incarceration or who formerly experienced incarceration. According to the most recent National Youth Risk Behavior Survey (Kann et al., 2017)—which studied a nationally representative sample of students in Grades 9–12 in public and private schools from all 50 states and the District of Columbia—2.4% of this sample reported being gay or lesbian and 8% reported being bisexual (Kann et al., 2018). The NYRBS does not ask questions related to gender identity, however in a recent study of almost 81,000 high school students (Grade 9–11) residing in Minnesota, results indicated that 2.7% of teens reported being transgender or gender nonconforming (Rider et al., 2018). In contrast, the percentage of both sexual minorities (those reporting being lesbian, gay, bisexual, or other) and gender minorities (transgender or gender non-conforming) in the juvenile incarceration system, is substantially higher. In a survey conducted by the U.S. Department of Justice on sexual victimization within the juvenile incarceration system, results indicated that a little over 12% of incarcerated juveniles reported being a sexual minority and were almost ten times more likely to report being sexually victimized while in detention (Beck et al., 2013). A more recent study of 200 adjudicated youth in seven juvenile incarceration facilities across the county showed that 20% of youth in detention halls were lesbian (L), gay (G), bisexual (B), questioning (Q), gender nonconforming (GNC), or transgender (T). Notably, 85% of those who identified as LGBQ/GNCT were youth of color (Irvine & Canfield, 2016). As one thinks about community college students, they are often more likely to be people of color, which has strong correlations with being targeted by the carceral system.

It is important to understand that involvement in the incarceration system exists at the intersection of race, socioeconomic status, gender identity, and sexuality. Consistent with this position, results in the aforementioned study (Irvine & Canfield, 2016) indicated that nearly 40% (39.9%) of girls in the juvenile carceral system reported being lesbian, bisexual, questioning, and/or gender nonconforming with the vast majority being girls of color (Irvine & Canfield, 2016). As mentioned in the previous section, queer and trans folks are also more likely to be involved in the child welfare system (Wilson et al., 2014). Consistent with this prior work, Irvine and Canfield (2016) also found that within the study sample LGBQ (lesbian, gay, bisexual, & questioning) incarcerated youth were three times more likely to have been removed from their home (30%) and seven times more likely to have been placed in a group or foster home (23%) than their straight counterparts (Irvine & Canfield, 2016).

Involvement with the adult carceral system for queer and trans adults is strikingly similar to that for juveniles. In a recent study conducted by researchers at the Williams Institute analyzing the National Inmate Survey (2011–2012; NIS-3), sexual minorities were incarcerated at much higher rates than would be expected by population estimates (Meyer et al., 2017). Consistent with the research on juvenile carceral involvement, this finding was particularly robust for women. Specifically, 42.1% of women in prison and 35.7% of women in jail self-identified as LGB (lesbian, gay, or bisexual)—or had same-sex sexual experience prior to incarceration (Meyer et al., 2017). It is important to remember that only 5.1% of women in the general population identify as LGBT (Newport, 2018). Although at this time it is not possible to obtain accurate counts of transgender and gender non-conforming folks experiencing incarceration, the National Inmate Survey *estimated* that there were approximately 3,209 transgender adults held in prisons or jails in the United States (Beck et al., 2013). Estimations of transgender carceral system involvement can also be gleaned from a study involving transgender veterans accessing care through the Veterans Administration. In this study, researchers found that transgender veterans were twice as likely to have been incarcerated or in an incarceration diversion program than non-transgender veterans (Brown & Jones, 2015). It is not currently possible to ascertain the percentage of adult incarcerated individuals who identify as gender non-conforming. Overall, research clearly indicates that queer and trans individuals are more likely to be impacted by the carceral system both as juveniles and adults.

In recent years, there has been a renewed interest by community colleges in providing educational opportunities to those individuals currently and/or formerly experiencing incarceration (Bukoski & Hatch, 2015). In terms of this education, the community college system is the primary provider of education within correctional facilities and for those who are formerly incarcerated. For example, in a recent study of institutions providing higher education in prison, roughly 60% were public 2-year institutions compared to only 20% for public 4-year institutions (Castro et al., 2018). One state that has taken the lead in the education of currently or formerly incarcerated students is California. The California Community College System has made progress due to legislative changes (The Public Safety and Rehabilitation Act of 2016) and the current leadership from the chancellor's office. Several factors that aided the progress included: specific guidance to the college system on limiting the use of carceral system history in hiring decisions for faculty and staff as well as for students seeking employment on campus (Office of General Counsel Advisory 2018-04), the development of grant programs to stimulate the creation of programs and service to serve this population (Office of General Counsel Advisory 2018-04), and finally, providing financial support to cover tuition (Community Colleges; California College Promise, A.B. 19 [2017]). Additionally, and importantly, the California Community College system is open access (acceptance is not based on prior academic performance or standardized test scores), has a lower cost of attendance, and the availability to participate in certificates or shorter-term programs. In a recent report from the nonprofit organization Corrections to College CA, over 40% of California Community College Respondents (college presidents and vice presidents) indicated that they had 50 or more formerly incarcerated students enrolled in a given semester (Corrections to College CA).

Issues Faced by Carceral System-Impacted Queer and Trans Students

The types of issues carceral system-impacted queer and trans students face can compound and vary widely. Some of the issues educators should be aware of are described below:

1. *Lack of employment opportunities*—Individuals who have experienced incarceration face bleak employment prospects (Couloute & Kopf,

2018). This is particularly challenging for trans and gender non-conforming formerly incarcerated students.
2. *Stigma*—Students with incarceration histories may find it more difficult to find support networks on community college campuses as they often face rejection and stigmatization for this part of their life story. It is imperative to create campus environments that are non-judgmental and recognize that incarceration is a symptom of larger issues of inequity faced by marginalized communities.
3. *Rejection of queer and trans identity within system-impacted support services*—Even within supportive and affirming system-impacted support services, queer and/or trans students may find it difficult to find support within these communities. The majority of formerly incarcerated students are male and masculine; thus, presenting queer and trans students who are female identified, feminine, gender non-conforming, or trans may find that spaces on campuses that support those who have experienced incarceration may not be spaces that are safe or accessible for these students.

Tips for Serving Queer and Trans System-Impacted Students

1. *Hire queer and trans system-impacted students!* It is imperative that any campuses that have programs that serve formerly incarcerated students or those campuses that have programs to serve queer and trans students should prioritize hiring folks from the community who have also experienced incarceration. At the system level, it is important that we prioritize hiring students who would in other situations have a difficult time obtaining employment. We have the opportunity to provide much needed employment and economic benefits to a group who otherwise would have few options. Colleges should understand that when they are welcoming carceral-impacted students they should aim to provide employment options and ensure they are LGBTQ+ inclusive.
2. *Establish a hiring process.* Hiring processes on campuses can be archaic and glacially slow at best! Owing to this slow pace, it may be impossible for these students to wait for college positions and must take any job offered to survive. Additionally, some colleges have policies that do not allow them to hire individuals with a carceral history. It is important that professionals work creatively to find ways to support these students. Some ideas include: investigating the possibility of using work study to hire students, paid internship programs, course credit internships, and collaborations with

community organizations. In this same vein it is imperative to be thoughtful about how and when these students will get paid. For example, most scarcely impacted queer and/or trans students will need to be paid on a regular schedule. It is unlikely that these students can work for long stretches without pay (e.g., if students are paid by stipend at the end of the semester).
3. *Mobilize the college.* Those professionals serving queer and trans system-impacted students must leverage every single opportunity to create allies, supporters, and champions of the work in all spaces of the college—from the librarians to the custodial staff, the financial aid department, the disabled student services department on campus, and especially the student mental health services department.
4. *Create networks of support.* In addition to creating support networks while the students are on campus, it is important to help develop opportunities for students once they transfer or leave campus. For example, are their programs at the local 4-year college that also support system-impacted students and are those spaces affirming of queer and trans formerly incarcerated students? Develop relationships with the counseling department, transfer department, and with the local business community to help facilitate internship and employment opportunities as well as formal and informal mentoring opportunities.

Students who have been or are incarcerated may be aiming to get involved with the LGBTQ+ community at the college; therefore, the community should be challenged to destigmatize and understand the carceral systems impact on LGBTQ+ people. Any program serving students who have been impacted by the carceral system should be trained on LGBTQ+ inclusion, and any program serving LGBTQ+ students should be trained on issues students who have been incarcerated face.

Homelessness, Food Insecurity, and Economic Disadvantage

Given that queer and trans individuals are overrepresented in both the foster care system and carceral system, it is perhaps of little surprise that queer and trans individuals are also overrepresented with people experiencing homelessness. In terms of youth homelessness, the 2015 LGBTQ Homeless Youth Provider Survey—which surveyed 138 agencies across the United States who specifically served the youth homeless population—reported that 85% of providers reported serving LGBTQ (lesbian, gay, bisexual, transgender, or questioning) youth. Of those service providers who reported serving queer and trans youth, LGBQ (lesbian, gay, bisexual, or questioning) youth accounted for 29% of the homeless youth they served and roughly 4% were transgender and genderqueer youth (Choi et al., 2015). Again, it is important to understand that these rates are substantially higher than the estimates of youth in the general population who report being LGBTQ (Wilson et al., 2014). Additionally, this study found that service providers report serving more LGBTQ youth over time and that these youth spent a longer time being homeless than their non-LGBTQ peers (Choi et al., 2015). Additionally, and importantly, as we consider the previous research on the foster care involvement for LGBTQ youth, in this study over half of the providers reported that the primary reason among their LGBTQ clients was due to being forced out by parents or running away because of their sexual orientation and/or gender identity. Consistent with the previous research reported, these traumas were more likely to be reported by LGBTQ POC (people of color), with African-American/Black and Latinx comprising roughly 45% of the reported LGBTQ homeless youth served (Choi et al., 2015).

In terms of adult homelessness, it is very difficult to ascertain the percent of the adult homeless population that identifies as queer. There has been slightly more work on transgender homelessness. For example, the U.S. Transgender Survey (USTS) reported that 30% of its 27,715 respondents had experienced homelessness at some point in their lives, with 12% having had such an experience within the past year (James et al., 2016). Transgender women of color experienced even higher rates of homelessness. For example, 51% of Black transgender women reported being homeless at some point in their lifetime. In the most recent Hope Center college survey (Goldrick-Rab et al., 2019), which assessed basic needs for college students, results showed that non-binary and transgender college students reported substantially higher homelessness rates than their cisgender counterparts. In fact, transgender college students had the highest rates of homelessness of any group of students studied (35%). Additionally, the results also showed that almost 25% of gay, lesbian, or bisexual college students were homeless in the previous year compared with 16% of heterosexual students. As one would expect, those who are more likely to experience homelessness are also more likely to experience food insecurity, meaning the students feared they would not have enough money to have an appropriate or adequate amount of food for themselves in the last month. Not surprisingly, compared with heterosexual and cisgender counterparts, those who reported being gay, lesbian, bisexual, transgender, and/or non-binary were far more likely to have these concerns. Again, community colleges are most likely to serve these homeless, housing unstable, and food insecure students and these students often have intersecting and overlapping needs. Results from the aforementioned #RealCollege survey (Goldrick-Rab et al., 2019) found that community college students were more likely to report being food insecure, housing insecure, or homeless in the past year in comparison to their 4-year counterparts (62% versus 51%). Community college students were also more likely to be both housing insecure and food insecure than those at a 4-year college (32% versus 20%). It is important to note that community college students are also far less likely to be able to benefit from on-campus housing and meal services.

As what can only be seen as a natural outcropping of the cumulative effects of trauma and disenfranchisement borne by the queer and trans community, research shows that LGBT individuals are more likely to live in poverty than their heterosexual cisgender counterparts (Badgett, Choi, & Wilson, 2019). Further analysis found that the highest rates of poverty were experienced by the transgender community, bisexual cisgender women, and LGBT individuals of color. For example, transgender individuals were 70% more likely to be in poverty than cisgender men and 38% more likely than cisgender women. Similar to research previously reported on vulnerabilities for bisexual cisgender women, the results showed that these women were more likely to experience poverty than either their heterosexual female or lesbian counterparts. Roughly 18% of heterosexual cisgender women and lesbian women met the definition of poverty for this study. In contrast, nearly 30% of cisgender bisexual women were poor. Additionally, as mentioned at the outset of this section, the influence of race on these outcomes cannot be overstated. Almost across the board, people of color had higher rates of poverty in comparison to their White counterparts. This effect is true when comparing the rates of poverty between LGBT POC and White cisgender heterosexual individuals but also when comparing LGBT people of color to White LGBT individuals. For example, 23.4% of White cisgender bisexual women were in poverty; however, the rate for Hispanic cisgender bisexual women was almost double (45.4%). Discrimination and marginalization do not happen within the context of a single identity but is cumulative across the identities individuals hold. To reiterate, homeless, food insecure, and economically disadvantaged students represent a larger portion of students on community college campuses versus on 4-year college campuses (Ma & Baum, 2016; Goldrick-Rabet al., 2019) and many of them will also be queer and trans students. When thinking about how to best serve queer and trans students we must also consider how we assist students with basic needs.

Issues Faced on Community College Campuses for Housing Insecure, Food Insecure, and Economically Disadvantaged Queer and Trans Students

1. *Cascading difficulties*—As the groundbreaking work of Abraham Maslow informs us, you cannot attend to higher level needs (love and belonging, esteem, and self-actualization) if your basic needs go unmet. Queer and trans students who cannot meet their basic needs, who struggle to feed themselves and their families, who are unhoused or under-housed, and who face economic uncertainty struggle to maintain attendance in school, to perform well in class, and to persist in their education.
2. *Safety*—As queer and trans students are experiencing homelessness they are often at risk of other types of crimes; for example, sleeping in ones car can leave someone in unsafe situations and their few belongings could be stolen.
3. *Mental health*—Students facing uncertainty and stress factors will have to navigate challenges with wellness and emotional and mental health issues.

Tips for Serving Homeless, Food Insecure, and Economically Disadvantaged Queer and Trans Students

1. *Basic needs center*—Some colleges have created basic needs centers that are a centralized location for students to access help with meeting their basic needs. Assistance includes help applying for food assistance; availability of emergency financial grants for students facing an unexpected need; as well as community resources for housing, food, or financial needs. It is imperative that these centers also be culturally competent in serving the queer and trans community. For example, if resources for shelters are provided for emergency housing, it is important to note that not all shelters honor lived identity and may reject or further harm trans gender or gender non-conforming students who seek out these shelters.
2. *Case management*—Students who cannot meet their basic needs can easily fall between the cracks of the student services support network. Case management involves consistent contact by a case manager with at-risk students who can be identified through the basic needs center. The case manager would be responsible for coordinating resources for the student both on campus and within the community.

3. *Food pantries and distributions*—Another important service to provide on campuses is a food pantry, food distribution, or grocery pick up. Food pantries generally involve nonperishable items (e.g., rice, pasta, canned beans) that students can "shop" from. Additionally, these pantries can provide sanitary items (e.g., tampons and pads) and other hygiene items; avoid assigning specific genders to the items. Food distributions are generally coordinated with local food banks and involve the distribution of fresh and perishable items (e.g., fruits & vegetables). An additional benefit of these food pantries and distributions is as a mechanism to identify students for case management. For queer and trans students, this can also be an opportunity to link them to the campus LGBTQ+ resources and center (if present).
4. *Financial aid*—At times, financial aid offices may require parents' tax documents. Many queer and trans youth have been excommunicated by parents, so they may not be able to complete financial aid documents. Financial aid offices should have a means to granting aid, even if a student cannot obtain parental tax documents.

Many colleges are improving their basic needs services, and as those offices become more robust they should be aware of the diversity of the students they serve. Basic needs centers must actively collaborate with LGBTQ+ services at the college and in the community.

Age, Work, Parenting, and Geographical Limitations

Additional populations to consider when developing programming to serve queer and trans community college students are older students, students working full time, geographically limited students, and student parents.

Older, Working, and/or Student Parents

When comparing the age of students at a 4-year university to a community college, 50% of enrolled students at 4-year public institutions are under 20 years. In comparison, only 21% of community college students are under 20. Additionally, over a quarter of community college students are 30 years of age or older and one-third of students work full time while in school and are twice as likely to have at least one dependent (Ma & Baum, 2016). It is important to note that research indicates that student parents are twice as likely as non-parenting students to be housing insecure and food insecure (Goldrick-Rab et al., 2019).

Key Issues Faced in Community Colleges for Queer and Trans Students Who Are Older, Working, and/or Parents

1. *Limited time*—Queer and trans students who are managing work and parenting have very limited time. These students are unlikely to have the schedule flexibility to attend traditional on- campus programming.
2. *Lack of issue representation*—The programming that is produced on community college campuses may not speak to our older students and they lack community and do not feel like they belong. Finding community and social support is key to success.

Tips for Serving Older, Working, and/or Student Parents

1. *Online resources and support.* Make sure you have a virtual presence as well as an on-campus presence. Remember that not all students access social media through the same portals, and it is important to be mindful of these differences in access.
2. *Speak to their lived experiences*—It is important to consider what older, working students, and student parents need in terms of resources and support.
3. *Families are diverse*—Remember, family forms in many different ways. Queer and trans communities can often make assumptions about the family make-up and lifestyle, so ensure that "family" is an inclusive term and idea.

Geographically Limited Students

Finally, and importantly, community college students are often geographically bound. Specifically, research by Hillman and Weichman (2016) found that community college students attend college on average of 31 miles from their home with a median of 8 miles. In contrast, those attending a public 4-year college attended school on average almost three times as far from home (82 miles), and those attending a private 4-year college on average 258 miles away (Hillman & Weichman, 2016). Many community college students attend a community college close to home for financial reasons and familial obligations. If community colleges are in rural or politically less welcoming environments, queer and trans students may have limited access to community-based organizations such as LGBTQ+ center. Many of these colleges are not near LGBTQ+ communities or community centers. In these scenarios, the college will be the primary access for support for these students.

Tips for Serving Geographically Limited Students
1. *Be the one stop shop*—Be mindful that the services on your campus may be the only access your students have to queer and trans support.
2. *Develop connections with community organizations*—In areas in which there are local community organizations, but students have limited transportation availability, consider how you might bring those organizations onto campus to serve students or provide virtual access to the resources and services.
3. *Utilize online and virtual resources*—When there is not the opportunity to gather in person, to bring famous speakers, or provide counseling or other QT specific services, find ways to virtually engage and share those resources.

Conclusion

In summary, queer and trans students on community college campuses are a diverse group of individuals with overlapping and intersecting identities and needs. Much of the early research on LGBTQ+ students in higher education have revolved around the needs of White, cisgender, middle-class, traditionally college-aged students; those are not the students at most of our community colleges. We acknowledge that the sections above do not fully encompass every aspect of identity and intersections in the lives of queer and trans people; this is a limitation. We hope that future scholars or our future selves will further explore disability, religion, immigration status, language, nationality, and other critical social identities. As we begin to delve deeper into how to serve these often-overlooked communities of students, it behooves us to keep the following at the forefront of our mind.

Students Live Intersectional Lives

People's lives and identities are not unidimensional, and we must understand that oppression is experienced differently by people with different lived experiences. For example, it is fundamentally a different experience to be a queer or trans student with a stable and loving home life than to have been kicked out and abandoned for your sexual orientation or gender identity.

Race Always Matters

There is no such thing as color blind. In our work, we must be race conscious and anti-racist! We must ensure that our work is not only welcoming and supportive of sexual orientation and gender identity but also of student's racial and ethnic identities. This book centers LGBTQ+ populations, but when talking about any oppressed group in the United States the cross section of race always amplifies challenges, violence, and discrimination.

Use Your Privilege Wisely

As professionals doing equity and social justice work, we must always ensure that we are centering the voices of our most marginalized. We must actively and consciously hold space for the narratives of queer and trans people of color who have been historically excluded from the conversation. Our privileged identities can leave gaps in what we know and how we know, so it is crucial to approach equity work with humility and center those marginalized identities we are not a part of.

Representation Matters

Make sure that your services, faculty, and your professionals are reflective of the faces and needs of the students that you serve. Collaborate across programs that serve marginalized students (e.g., multicultural spaces, first-generation programs, basic needs programs, disability support services, etc.). Challenge your college on hiring! There has been more discussion on recruiting BIPOC faculty, which is a critical place to start. Workplaces should continue to expand efforts of recruiting intersectional and marginalized employees. Moreover, institutions and organizations must also support them when they join the institutions.

Build Connection

At the end of the day, this work is based on connections built between the college and the students. Each college should seek to build a warm, supportive, non-judgmental space for queer and trans students on your campus. This space can be physical or virtual, but it is absolutely necessary that students are able to build an authentic relationship(s) with the individuals doing this work. The value of social spaces to just relax, eat lunch, and build community are vital to student success and, at times, survival.

4

Institutionalizing LGBTQ Efforts

> *Like racism and all forms of prejudice, bigotry against transgender people is a deadly carcinogen. We are pitted against each other in order to keep us from seeing each other as allies. Genuine bonds of solidarity can be forged between people who respect each other's differences and are willing to fight their enemy together. We are the class that does the work of the world and can revolutionize it. We can win true liberation.*
>
> —Leslie Feinberg (1992, p. 22)

Many community colleges are planning to create institutionalized LGBTQ+ services and centers. The term "center" is often used in regard to the name of a physical space and for the "centering" of LGBTQ+ people; however, it can also refer to the staff, programs, and services dedicated to serving LGBTQ+ people. Over the last 2 decades, we have been instrumental in creating LGBTQ+ services from scratch, as well as redeveloping and restructuring centers at numerous community colleges and 4-year institutions. This section will provide insights and recommendations as institutions establish LGBTQ+ services. The recommendations also include insights from the survey of community colleges that have existing LGBTQ+

services. Each institution will have unique challenges, histories, resources, and successes. This is not a comprehensive list but will provide considerations and guidance to establish programs and services that impact success for LGBTQ+ students.

This section offers wisdom from the initial concept to building allies and accomplices to getting board approval for a new center, service model, or program. Examples of the challenges faced by pioneers of established centers will be shared through multiple resources. In the current context, many educators continue to be overwhelmed with how to get the ball rolling when it comes to providing services for the LGBTQ+ community due to the continued systemic oppression by the design of the organization and the biases of individuals who lead them. This chapter will provide specific details for the impact on your campus and community.

LGBTQ+ centers are still relatively new to community colleges and getting approval to start a center or services is one of the first big challenges. We aimed to understand how the colleges with existing centers and services got started. Some of the colleges shared that it was a long process that took up to 10 years. Most of the efforts were faculty-driven, but a few colleges shared that students mobilized and brought requests and plans to senior administrators. One colleges' center began after a notable hate incident occurred, and students demanded the college take action. Another college created an LGBTQ Center after the national tragedy with the Pulse Nightclub shooting in Orlando that targeted and killed patrons at an LGBT club.

Most of the colleges started with a steering committee or task force to address the needs of LGBTQ+ students, and that evolved into paid staff members and a center. Several colleges had faculty and staff who began offering Ally Trainings (LGBTQ+ inclusion training) on their own, and as an outcropping of these trainings, allies and accomplices on campus grew in number. Educating the college about the issues and needs led to the masses supporting an LGBTQ+ center or program. Most colleges had a student organization at the college before a formal center or program began. Having a committee, Ally Trainings, and a student organization creates multiple stakeholders at the college to give input and push for formal services. Overall, the groups petitioning for formal LGBTQ+ services were successful when they tied their proposal to retention and graduation efforts. Securing data on disproportionate impact can be challenging, but can be a valuable tool to secure resources, staff positions, and establish institutional efforts. If you struggle to find ways to get the data on LGBTQ+ students or employees, a campus climate study may be another way to generate other types of data—both quantitative and qualitative—to use to communicate to senior leaders at the college.

Creating Missions, Vision, and Program Goals

In order to get the approval for an LGBTQ+ center some type of mission or vision should have been drafted, but once the establishment begins, this should be revisited and refined. As the college begins to plan for an LGBTQ+ center (whether a physical center or institutionalized services) the mission, vision, and goals must be clarified. There are many issues that LGBTQ+ students, employees, and community members face, and a community college will not be able to address every need. The ultimate goal of the college is to successfully graduate and transfer students. There are many life situations and identity specific challenges that will impact an LGBTQ+ students' ability to succeed. Oftentimes, the outside of the classroom challenges can have huge impacts on whether an LGBTQ+ student succeeds; however, the college may have little it can do to address those societal injustices. The purpose statement should name the issues with as much specificity and research as possible.

The mission should be grounded in why the college wants to serve LGBTQ+ students and how that connects to the institutional mission. The missions should balance a global vision of addressing homophobia and transphobia, but be more specifically focused on how those –isms show up in higher education and a community college. The vision should revolve around the long-term hope of how this new effort will impact LGBTQ+ people at the college. Much of this will likely be discussed with the group pushing for proposed services, and all people will not agree. We have seen a variety of identity-based offices create missions and visions that are broader and fit more into a nonprofit community center model. Overall, the mission and vision should complement and drill down from the college mission and vision.

The program goals are how the LGBTQ+ center will get to the mission and vision. What will the center actually do to improve the retention, course success, and graduation/transfer rates of LGBTQ+ students? We recommend identifying four to six program goals that are broader and have been measured and proven to get LGBTQ+ centers towards achieving its mission. The college must decide on who it will serve primarily and secondarily, and what services should be provided. The program goals often could be simplified to community building for students; advocacy, mentoring, and coaching for students; LGBTQ+ education of college employees; and policy and procedure analysis and development.

Audiences and Services

All of the centers surveyed had the central focus of serving students. Most of the colleges also had secondary audiences of employees. Serving LGBTQ+

employees can be a useful strategy in order to increase diversity of employees, which in turn adds to curriculum inclusion, mentorship opportunities for students, and representation at the college. Additionally, some of the focus on employees were related to discrimination and harassment policies. All of the colleges who responded included sexual orientation and gender identity in protected groups for employees. The recent SCOTUS decision (*Bostock v. Clayton County, Georgia*, 2020) held that laws protecting individuals from employment discrimination applied to transgender employees. Based on this ruling, sexual orientation and gender identity should be included as protected groups across all colleges.

The services provided by the LGBTQ+ centers were mostly consistent across the institutions. The main services provided included:

- *Social and educational programs*: A significant part of college success is finding connections to others, and that often might come from "getting involved" at the college. This social engagement leads to more successful students (Astin, 1984), and hosting social opportunities allows LGBQT+ students to connect with other students at the college in order to create a support system and connection to the college. Attending social events also allows students the opportunity to connect with faculty and staff and better understand how to access college resources. Social programs often were movie screenings, orientation programs, dance parties, drag shows, bingo, and video game events.

    In addition to social programs, most centers hosted educational events. The educational event could be college-wide in order to provide awareness and knowledge to heterosexual and/or cisgender people at the college. The educational events could also be for those in the LGBTQ+ community since many in this community do not have access to their own histories, news, or in-depth knowledge of the diversity of the LGBTQ+ community. Educational programs often were guest lectures, documentary screenings, workshops about intersectionality, and workshops on social movements, social justice, and activism.

    Many centers have annual programs that occur across the country or even the world. Annual events could include Lavender Graduation, to recognize the accomplishments of LGBTQ+ who are graduating and/or transferring despite facing additional obstacles. Annual awareness building events including Transgender Day of Remembrance, International Transgender Day of Visibility, National Coming Out Day, Pride events, Spirit Day focused on

ending bullying and harassment, and National Day of Silence focused on ending the silencing and erasure of LGBTQ+ people.
- *Student organizations*: The centers helped create, guide, and support the student organizations. The LGBTQ center and services staff would find other faculty and staff to support the club and were often involved if the club was struggling or needed assistance with mediation or crisis situations.
- *Advocacy*: Unfortunately, LGBTQ+ people in higher education continue to face hate and bias incidents and crimes, and often they do not know where to turn to for support and guidance. LGBTQ+ centers can provide first-line support and knowledge on how to navigate complex reporting processes.
- *Support groups by identities*: In addition to providing formal student organizations, many centers also offered support groups by identities for students to gather, discuss, and provide peer support. The support groups included trans and non-binary groups; Black, indigenous, and other queer and trans people of color; womyn and femmes; masculine of center; queer and religious; and bi, pansexual, and fluid.
- *Mentorship programs*: Several colleges had formal mentorship programs for LGBTQ+ students. The mentorship could be pairing a new student with a more senior LGBTQ+ student or pairing a student with a faculty or staff member. Mentorship programs were helpful for centers with very small staffs in order to spread the work across the college.
- *Training for employees*: A core service at most of the colleges was providing LGBTQ+ training to employees at the college. The common title was often "Ally Training" or "Safe Zone" training. The overall goal of this training is to provide awareness, knowledge, and skills to employees both inside and outside of the classroom to ensure college employees can effectively serve and educate LGBQT+ people. Some colleges had train-the-trainer programs and many people at the college offered these workshops. There was a consistent theme of college wanting this to be mandatory; however, none of the colleges were successful with mandatory employee training. Some colleges had multiple workshops that went beyond the basics. As mentioned above, the recent SCOTUS decision held that laws protecting individuals from employment discrimination applied to transgender employees. Additionally, a recent federal appeals court decision has held that Title IX protects the rights of transgender students (*Adams*

v. School Board of St. Johns County, Florida, 2020). These two cases provide a strong argument that training regarding sexual orientation and gender identity should be included in the mandatory sexual harassment training provided on campuses.

- *Employee support*: Several of the colleges aimed to provide support to LGBTQ+ employees. Some centers helped transgender and non-binary employees navigate changing names and pronouns and understand benefits. Only a few colleges had formal employee resource groups (ERGs). ERGs have become common in other industries and at some higher education institutions. Most ERGs are focused on race; however, several colleges had LGBTQ+ ERGs. The ERGs were mostly social in nature, but at times they did serve in advocacy roles for the larger LGBTQ+ community.
- *Support changing names, gender, and pronouns*: A common challenge for transgender and non-binary people are databases, software programs, and rosters with names and genders. Most of the LGBTQ+ centers led the college with creating policies, protocols, and practices so LGBTQ+ students and employees could change their name, gender, and pronouns. Some of the places they needed support were with IDs, emails, class rosters, learning management systems, and records such as diplomas and transcripts.
- *Facilities*: LGBTQ+ center staff were often the ones to initiate changes to facilities, so they were more inclusive and safer for transgender and non-binary people. Most colleges had gender-neutral restrooms, but it was still a struggle for most to have them across the college and in locations close enough for students and employees. A struggle that most colleges still had were related to providing gender-inclusive locker rooms and shower spaces within athletic and physical education programs. A common concern for colleges is how to retrofit existing buildings and structures to make them more inclusive. This scenario requires a great deal of creativity and "out of the box" thinking. Additionally, however, it is important that the needs of transgender and non-binary people on campus be considered in the plans and contracts for new buildings.
- *Queer studies classes*: Several institutions had queer studies courses that were connected to the centers. It was often the faculty employee of the center teaching it and/or the center helped recruit students to participate in the course. Taking academic courses around LGBTQ+ studies can be transformative for students; in a prior study about LGBTQ+ Christian students (Johnson, 2012),

students who took critical theory courses had more resilience and determination when having self-harming thoughts.
- *LGBTQ+ library*: Centers often gathered LGBTQ+ focused films, books, zines, and other media to provide to students. Often students struggled to find LGBTQ+ centered media, so centers were able to provide resources. The efforts were in collaboration with libraries at some colleges, but having a check-out option in the LGBTQ+ center was a useful strategy for those who were not comfortable checking out these materials at the general library.
- *Financial support*: LGBTQ+ people are more likely to experience homelessness, underemployment and unemployment and be financially at risk (Badgett et al., 2019). Many LGBTQ+ centers provided necessary financial support to students. Many had scholarships for LGBTQ+ students. Some centers offered textbook support. Many of the centers collaborated with basic needs and food banks in order to support LGBTQ+ students' basic needs.
- *Sexual and menstrual products*: LGBTQ+ centers often provide sexual health products such as condoms, lube, and dental dams. LGBTQ+ youth are often not taught sexual health that is inclusive of their identities or bodies. Additionally, their sexual desires and practices have often been shamed in society. LGBTQ+ centers aimed to destigmatize sexuality and educate on how to practice safer sex. One college also provided menstrual products as they understand that transgender men or other masculine people with a menstrual cycle may have complications around menstruating and feeling safe getting products.

Each college's LGBTQ+ center or program may have slightly different goals or services depending on community and focus. If students, employees, or community members push for new services, they should be evaluated against the mission, vision, and program goals.

Involving the Stakeholder

Each college has stakeholders who have influence and are needed for new initiatives to be successful. As a new project is being developed, the stakeholders should be identified. Once they are identified it is crucial to anticipate any opposition and find ways to address those and build trust and collaborations. For most colleges, the faculty are key stakeholders. Likely this would include the academic senate as well as other influential faculty. There will also be those who oppose LGBTQ+ support; however, we encourage you to find faculty who have been long-term supporters of LGBTQ+ efforts before there were any institutional efforts. Ensure they are consulted, included, and ask them to provide historical context and ideas. They may also be very helpful in illuminating the roadblocks to establishing services on the campus.

A key need is ensuring classrooms are inclusive, which requires faculty to gain awareness, knowledge, and skills. Faculty need to be understanding and supportive of LGBTQ+ issues in order for students to succeed in the classroom. Building allies and accomplices in the faculty will support transformation of campus climate at a much quicker rate.

Compliance officers such as Title IX officers, equal employment officers, and conduct officers all have a vested interest (or should) in understanding and improving climate for LGBTQ+. If LGBTQ+ services is involved with advocacy, they will need to work close and collaboratively with compliance officers. Students and employees who experience mistreatment due to sexual or gender identity will often tell their trusted LGBTQ+ professional before going to the compliance officer.

Students are obviously the most significant stakeholder, but they are often not consulted and included in establishing new efforts. The student government can be a significant supporter and sounding board. Many campuses also have an LGBTQ+ student organization, and they should be given multiple opportunities to consult and advise. If there is an advisory group or implementation team there should be student representation, and those students should be compensated for their work.

Another stakeholder is local LGBTQ+ organizations. If the city or local area has an LGBTQ+ center, aim to involve them in many ways. A college LGBTQ+ center can partner and outsource many services (such as STI and STD testing) to the local community centers. A community college partnership outside of academia are critical for recruiting students, employees, and ensuring efforts outside of college walls are also connected to the college.

Getting Data

As one is proposing a new center or establishing the new center, having adequate data is crucial. Most colleges say they make data-driven decisions, yet much of the time they do not have adequate data on different populations. We suggest working closely with the institutional research office and the admissions office to collect this information. Some states and districts already include questions about gender identity and sexual orientation in admissions applications, employment applications, and/or climate study surveys. If this is not collected, it creates a substantial obstacle to gain data to use as supporting evidence in a proposal or as insight to understand issues and measure progress.

If the institution is collecting information about gender identity and sexual orientation in applications, it should understand the complications with terminology when asking. The Consortium of Higher Education LGBT Resource Professionals provides a best practice guide to asking about sexual orientation and gender identity. Also recognize that many younger adults are coming to terms with their identities and the data collected at application is often an underestimate of the actual population of LGBTQ+ people at the college. It is also important to understand that many colleges only collect this type of demographic data at the initial application and never again. Still others have age restrictions on asking questions regarding sexual orientation and gender identity. For example, some college systems require that the application be over the age of 18 in order for the questions to be presented. At times, parents or guardians may be completing the college application, and the student has not shared their sexual or gender identity with the parent or guardian. Taken together, this means that if data is even collected it may be woefully inaccurate, a fact that many administrators and executives are unaware of.

In addition to collecting info on admissions applications and employment applications, it is important to examine the experiences of LGBTQ+ and other marginalized people at the college; a great example of this is the study: *State of Higher Education for LGBT People* (Rankin et al., 2010; Garvey et al., 2015). When conducting surveys and climate studies, ask questions about gender and sexual identities. This information can be further analyzed with intersecting communities to understand unique issues or patterns affecting within the LGBTQ+ community by race, ability, religion, immigration status, and other identities. In addition to quantitative data, qualitative data is a powerful way to give voice to students and allow them to tell their own stories. Hosting in-depth interviews and focus groups can provide insight to the direction of the services as providing a sense of empowerment and community building for the LGBTQ+ people at the college. In order to have adequate data, a trusting and sharing process should be established between admissions, the research office, and the LGBTQ+ staff.

If college-level data cannot be acquired or utilized, we recommend using national data to support the issues students are facing and for interventions that will support LGBTQ+ to persist and succeed. Many community college research offices are understaffed and the LGBTQ+ center staffing is often minimal, so gaining primary research is often a luxury that community colleges don't have. A literature review of national research can often be a sufficient substitute for college specific data. Some needs and narratives are not easy to articulate through White-dominant and capitalistic research approaches, but using these tools can support goals and direction depending on the institutional culture.

Staffing and Hiring

Once an LGBTQ+ center or program moves from being a proposal or a committee to being an institutionalized center or program, decisions will need to be made on who will do this work. Community college staffing models vary widely based on institutions with a consistent theme being "there is never enough people or hours to accomplish what is needed." Having adequate personnel to achieve the goals of an LGBTQ+ center is a constant struggle at nearly every institution, both community colleges and 4-year institutions. A simple recommendation is that an LGBTQ+ center should be staffed by multiple full-time professionals as well as student employees. A center that is aiming to shift cultural climates, lead college-wide efforts, and examine and create policy, should come with the recognition and title to do this level of work. An administrator at a director level will aid significance and the skills and authority to make critical change. This person should be at the level to shift an entire institution's climate. In addition to an empowered administrator, there should also be someone directly supporting students as well as staffing to train faculty and staff. Unfortunately, very few community colleges have a staffing model to effectively shift a college's climate and support all the students in need.

Although not required or legally enforceable, it is hugely beneficial if the people in these paid LGBTQ+ roles are a part of the LGBTQ+ community. They should have adequate professional and academic experience related to the role and population and not just be placed in the role because they are the only "gay" person at the institution. In addition to just the employee's gender and/or sexual identity, it is beneficial if the the team is diverse with other identities. Historically, LGBT centers have been staffed by mostly White, cisgender, gay and lesbian people. Trans people, people of color, and other identities named in Chapter 3 should be working LGBTQ+ centers or programs, which will allow students to connect with college employees who have similar lived experiences.

Common Staffing Models at Community Colleges

In the survey we completed of community colleges with existing LGBTQ+ efforts, we found insightful information on how these colleges chose to staff their center as well as what division of the college they were placed in an organizational structure. LGBTQ+ centers on college campuses vary in where they are housed in an organizational chart. Most of the centers and/or efforts were in student affairs; however, a few were in academic affairs or a diversity and equity division. The staffing levels varied; on the smaller end were efforts or centers that were staffed by part-time staff members or part-time faculty reassignment. The more robust staffed centers included a faculty member, a staff member, a mental health counselor, and student staff members. Most of the centers were staffed with one person and a combination of volunteers, part-time staff, and student assistants. About half of the staff members had multiple assignments, such as serving LGBTQ+ students and UndocuScholars (undocumented, DACA, and/or students coming from mixed-status families). It was less common for a community college center to have a director or someone at a manager level, which is often a strategy of many 4-year institutions. The challenge with the community college model is that the faculty employee is often not hired to do LGBTQ+ work—perhaps does not have the knowledge or skills either—and the staff member working in the center often is not in a position to create guidance or direction nor at the table to advocate for LGBTQ+ students' needs. A benefit of a tenured faculty member in a leadership role is that they can push for change without fear of dismissal or negative employment consequences.

A common gap with the community college centers and services was around mental health. Numerous colleges aimed to provide mental health support to LGBTQ+ students, but it was a common struggle. One college had a mental health therapist as a part-time staff member. Other centers had guest therapists who would host group sessions on a regular basis. Numerous colleges in California had academic and personal counselors assigned to LGBTQ+ centers; those counselors offered academic guidance and personal support with other needs and referrals to mental health therapists in the community.

A common strategy to further support LGBTQ+ efforts is including those beyond being full-time paid staff or faculty. Many centers had employees as volunteers who advised student organizations, mentored students, or hosted workshops. Several colleges had advisory groups or committees of other college employees who would provide insight, direction, and some minimal services. Additional staffing often came from interns or practicum students at nearby graduate programs and volunteers in the community. Many graduate students need experience and pathways to enter community college LGBTQ+ services, so it was easy to secure competent graduate students.

Significant contributions came from student staff members. Many had student volunteers or interns who got course credit; however, it is recommended that students be paid for their labor. An additional challenge with LGBTQ+ center efforts is ensuring staff are diverse and representative of the student population regarding race, ability, gender, religion, and other intersecting identities. Having only one or two employees limits colleges, so using students to represent diverse communities and give voice to often marginalized people within the LGBTQ+ community can be a useful strategy. Paying attention to identity and presentation is key to identity-based student services, but it can also lead to tokenization. Adding voice and perspective is essential; however, one student from a marginalized background cannot be the spokesperson for their entire community. Student voice and perspective are valuable; however, including student narratives and qualitative findings should be complemented with other national research and quantitative findings.

Student staffing in LGBTQ+ centers creates an intense sense of belonging for those working in the center and creates intentional mentorship opportunities for the student staff. Empowering student staff to identify needs in their community and guiding them to create solutions can build confidence and skills to guide them in their academic and career path. It is also important to note that some students, particularly those who identify as transgender and/or gender non-conforming face difficulties in obtaining employment on the open market (Grant et al., 2011). Student staff positions can be a wonderful opportunity for students to learn valuable work skills in a supportive and affirming environment—allowing them to build their work history and develop connections that may lead to additional employment opportunities outside of the college. Most of the centers who identified having student staff utilized them to perform basic office functions, but also to create social and educational efforts for their peers. LGBTQ+ centers must include students in some way. Whether as student leaders, volunteers, or paid staff members—preferred approach—the voice of students is crucial to success.

Hiring Considerations

The staff operating the LGBTQ+ center should be hired specifically for this role if possible. Working as a director, faculty coordinator, or staff member in an LGBTQ+ center requires specific knowledge and skill set. Beyond general higher education and student affairs administration skills, these employees must have in-depth knowledge of LGBTQ+ identity development, intersectional work with other identities, crisis response skills, healing and advocacy skills, and training and development skills. Some colleges often place faculty or staff who are part of the LGBTQ+ community but lack academic backgrounds and experience with LGBTQ+ people. Ill-equipped employees can do more harm than good. LGBTQ+ students have higher experiences of homelessness, suicide attempts and completions, substance abuse, and hate crimes and bias. Highly knowledgeable employees should be placed in these roles and on-going training and development should be supported.

Budgets and Funding

As a college aims to set up an LGBTQ+ center, funding should be discussed. The expenses can vary widely, but similar to staffing, nearly every college LGBTQ+ center will acknowledge that funding is a constant challenge. The majority of funds often go to salaries and personnel. Other costs are often associated with supplies, events and guest speakers or trainers, and travel to professional development conferences.

In the survey to the community college LGBTQ+ centers, the responders shared where their funds came from and some useful information. The funding of community college LGBTQ+ efforts is a constant struggle, and most identified this as a challenge to fully meet student needs. Our goal was to understand how the LGBQT+ centers got funding. Since many of the colleges surveyed were in California and the state provides community colleges equity funds to aid in reducing the opportunity gap, this was a regular source of funding. Most of the California colleges stated the majority of their funding came from state allocated equity funds. Other colleges stated they received general funds and/or student fees to support LGBTQ+ efforts. Many colleges also solicited donations to provide services and scholarships to students.

Space and Centers

Another decision as a college gets started is where this center or office will be located. The idea of space, place, facilities, and centers have significant meaning for communities who have struggled to find a place to belong and to feel safe and included. Most of the colleges surveyed had some type of space designated as a queer and trans inclusive space. Only about half of the institutions had a space completely dedicated to LGBTQ+ centers, where others had joint spaces. Some of the shared spaces included: a multicultural space that was also dedicated for LGBTQ+ students, a space for UndocuScholars and LGBTQ+ people, or a space that was a general equity center, which included anyone from a marginalized or oppressed background.

A consistent theme for those without spaces was to acquire a designated LGBTQ+ space since even in shared equity spaces many LGBTQ+ students did not feel included or comfortable being "out." For those who did have designated spaces, there was often fear that the space might be taken away and/or the space they had was too small and could not be used as a community gathering space. LGBTQ+ people have often lived in fear of being "outed," verbally harassed, and/or physically assaulted, so having a space that is intentional and named is necessary for complete inclusion, but also is a monumental symbol of value and inclusion.

Space has long been a challenge on college campuses, and marginalized communities have felt the literal marginalization that comes with fighting for scarce resources. The unknowns of how the COVID-19 pandemic may drastically adjust how higher education and college campuses function, but at present time, space and community building is critical. All oppressed and marginalized communities should have a physical space to feel safe and included until the entire college is actually a welcoming, safe, and inclusive place for marginalized people. However, some oppressed groups who have different levels of visibility, such as undocumented people and transgender people, have critical needs to be in a space they know is 100% accepting and affirming of their identities. A physical space with adequate signage is symbolic to LGBTQ+ people's existence and significant in acknowledging them as part of the college community.

Policies and Protocols

A key part of LGBTQ+ institutional efforts include ensuring policies and protocols are inclusive of LGBTQ+ people and provide protection for them. As a center gets started, it should do a deep dive and audit of nearly every policy and procedure at the college. Of course, this takes time and likely will never happen fully, but it is a long-term goal. Analyzing institutional and departmental policies and procedures can be risky, and it is easy to become the social justice police or the "gay police" who is always telling people they are not good enough. This work should be done in partnership if possible and should be done as the center builds allies and accomplices. There are several areas that a center should start with that often negatively impacts LGBTQ+ people:

- *Employee discrimination*: Some colleges may have the LGBTQ+ center staff members serve in a formal role that deals with LGBTQ+ employees reporting discrimination or mistreatment. It is crucial to understand this role and expectation. Laws vary state-by-state,

so colleges should know if their state includes sexual orientation and/or gender identity as protected groups.
- *Non-discrimination policies*: Colleges have non-discrimination policies that include protected groups. Even if the state the college is in does include LGBTQ+ people—sometimes gender identity or expression are not included—the institution can expand the groups included in the non-discrimination policy.
- *Bias and hate reporting*: LGBTQ+ are often targets of hate crimes and bias incidents, but there are many barriers to reporting on a college campus. Students may not know what a hate crime or bias incident is. They may not know how to report or to whom. They may be afraid to report or may not be "out" about their gender identity and/or sexual orientation. Creating a cohesive bias and hate reporting process is a significant project that involves many people. LGBTQ+ centers may have to start the conversation or at least be a part of the conversations to create policies and procedures. Title IX officers should understand how LGBTQ+ identities fit under the legal definition of sex discrimination.
- *Name and gender changes*: A significant challenge that students and employees may face is having their name and gender match their gender identity in the many records at a college. For employees, this can include their identification card, email name, college directory, and web site information. Ensure the college has a process for employees to change this with ease and share it with current and incoming employees. For students this can include student email names; class rosters; student identification cards; learning management systems; and official documents such as transcripts, financial aid documents, and diplomas. Some of the financial aid documents may require a legal name and gender change. Creating policies and procedures for name and gender changes is critical to the safety of transgender and non-binary people at the college. "Outing" someone could put their lives at risk since transgender people experience violence and harassment at alarming rates on college campuses (Rankin et al., 2010).

Communication and Outreach

LGBTQ+ centers should quickly create a communication plan. One of the first challenges is reaching the LGBTQ+ students. Even if the college does collect this information at admissions, it is often far underreported and difficult to access. When trying to reach other minoritized groups, such as by race, colleges have close to accurate lists of students to reach out to and offer services. It is a challenge to communicate with LGBTQ+ students, so intense and well-developed marketing plans should be used to engage students with the LGBTQ+ center. The center should partner with the marketing and public relations office to ensure they can reach as many students as possible. One way this can be accomplished is by sending initial communication to the entire student body and then begin to create a mailing list of interested students. It also cannot be stated enough the importance of using social media to reach our students. We must meet folks where they are and our younger students are on social media!

Another aspect of communication that should be developed focuses on crisis response. Unfortunately, there will be college, local, or national tragedies involving LGBTQ+ people, and the center should work with the senior administration and the public relations office to issue statements, plans, and actions the college will take. We recommend the college have draft statements prepared and agreed upon before the crisis occurs. Nearly every college has anti-LGBTQ+ protestors who come to the campus and make hurtful statements against LGBTQ+ people. These statements are often protected by the First Amendment, but the college should still have a response. A comprehensive communication plan should be put into effect when anti-LGBTQ+ protestors arrive at the college. Sadly, these are often good opportunities to reach LGBTQ+ students who seek support and reassurance during these difficult times. While it pains all of us that students are harmed by these interactions with protestors, it can also offer a unique opportunity to connect in a meaningful way with LGBTQ+ students on campus.

The LGBTQ+ global community celebrates and honors some specific events each year, and it can be beneficial for an LGBTQ+ center to communicate and organize around them. Audiences may be more receptive due to larger societies marketing LGBTQ+-focused events. Pride month in June has become almost a national celebration. National Coming Out Day is in October. Transgender Day of Remembrance is in November, and International Transgender Day of Visibility is in March.

Understanding Socio-Political Climates

One thing to count on is resistance. If we are trying to shift an entire culture and climate, we should expect resistance. Each college, region, state, and community are different. As a college aims to create an LGBTQ+ center, some will oppose. There may be opposition by students, employees, board members, alumni, and community members. Students may not want their student fees funding LGBTQ+ efforts. Employees may resist attending training about LGBTQ+ people. Local religious or hate groups may protest and challenge the efforts. We recommend anticipating each resistance and creating a plan of how you will address it. The center of these actions should be caring for the LGBTQ+ people at the college. Resistance to some at the college may just be an obstacle to work projects. However, resistance to someone in the LGBTQ+ community may trigger trauma, rejection, self-hatred, and leave them feeling unwanted, devalued, and fearful for their own safety.

Challenges

A community college establishing formal LGBTQ+ services or a center does not come without challenges. With real change comes real resistance. The colleges who completed the survey shared a variety of challenges as they began their LGBTQ+ efforts—challenges they were still facing. Some of the most common challenges when trying to start a center included:

- *No data*: Colleges are pressured to be data-driven, but most colleges do not collect data on LGBTQ+ students or employees. This produced obstacles for committees to justify that there was a need. Many colleges conducted surveys on their college and used national data to show there was a need related to LGBTQ+ students and campus climate, retention, and graduation.
- *Lack of awareness*: Many if not most employees on some of the colleges had no awareness of queer and trans identities nor the challenges people in these communities face. It was often a struggle to begin a conversation because people did not even have a basic understanding. Some colleges avoided this challenge because they hosted Ally Trainings for many employees before they proposed a formal center.
- *Resistance*: When advocating for historically marginalized and oppressed groups, there will be resistance. Many colleges faced resistance in subtle ways or in overt ways that condemned LGBTQ+ people. Resistance came from the local community where it was socially and politically opposed to LGBTQ+ rights. Some resistance came from other equity programs who were going to be asked to share spaces, staffing, and budgets. Identity politics and hierarchies of oppression created challenging dialogues for many colleges; much of community college conversations about equity focused on race alone. LGBTQ+ efforts added an additional layer

of identities and at times it complicated the conversations and efforts of college equity programs.
- *Lack of physical space*: Most colleges do not have vacant spaces just sitting, so creating a new LGBTQ+ space meant someone had to move. Finding adequate space was a very common challenge. When spaces were shared with other marginalized groups it often put multiple oppressed groups competing for resources. It is common for institutions and society to pit marginalized groups against each other, and those groups can further impose ideas of White supremacy, patriarchy, and capitalism that harm.

Once centers were created, the challenges continued. At the point of the survey, most of the community college centers were only a few years old. Any new program will face obstacles creating a foundation and structure. However, these community college LGBTQ+ centers struggled to find support and guidance. Some of the challenges facing the centers once established included:

- *Lack of funding*: Many colleges' senior administrators were supportive or neutral on the idea of LGBTQ+ efforts; however, even once approved, funding did not always follow. Most colleges that completed the survey stated that funding was a challenge to get started and continue. Funding to hire sufficient staffing made it difficult to provide services that meet students' needs. One center said it started being fully staffed by volunteers. Other centers do not have secure funding, so each year they must propose a budget and each year the funding appropriated is different. It is difficult to plan when the center does not know what the staffing model will be or what resources it has for student workers, programs, supplies, or services.
- *Measuring impact*: Limited access to data continued to challenge centers since they were expected to show how their services impacted course success, retention, and graduation and transfer rates. This remains a challenge since many colleges do not collect sexual orientation and gender identity as demographics similar to race, ethnicity, or sex. Some colleges did collect this information, but the institutional research office and the LGBTQ+ centers did not have collaborative relationships to produce useful data.
- *Outreach to students*: Many colleges struggled to communicate to students that there was an LGBTQ+ center, what they do, and how to access it. Part of this challenge stems from not having adequate lists of LGBTQ+ students. LGBTQ+ students are often still

coming to terms with their identities and some of these identities can be fluid. Additionally, the center's staffing was often small and not staffed to manage marketing and outreach functions.

Despite many challenges getting a center started and keeping it actively supporting students, the LGBTQ+ centers found ways to mentor, support, and advocate for students. It took time to establish a community and culture of inclusion for LGBTQ+ students and employees, but after just a short amount of time most of the colleges were proud of their centers and the work they were doing to create a campus focused on equity, justice, and liberation.

Conclusion and Successes

There will be many challenges as a college aims to create an LGBTQ+ center and provide crucial services to students while also trying to shift institutions grounded in heterosexism and cis-normativity; however, there are some happy and proud moments that our community colleges shared in their survey responses. The colleges surveyed about their LGBTQ+ efforts had numerous successes and strategies as they created spaces for students. Overall, the focus of the centers was to create a sense of community. A sense of community yields results—retention, degrees, course success, and healthy and happy students. Colleges wanted LGBTQ+ students to know they mattered, and once they knew they mattered, it shifts a campus climate (Schlossberg, Lynch, & Chickering, 1989). LGBTQ+ centers should go beyond just a focus on academic success. Equity in education is deeply tied to liberation and justice. As community colleges, the focus is on educational attainment; however, as colleges aim to focus on equity, they must see the larger societal pictures of injustice and aim for liberation of marginalized and oppressed groups.

Another success tip is to ensure all LGBTQ+ efforts have an understanding and intersectional approach. LGBTQ+ are not simply a sexual orientation or gender identity. Services and programs must consider how those identities show up for people of color, people with disabilities, religious minorities, poor and working class, older students, student parents, formerly incarcerated students, undocumented students, as well as many others who make up the diversity of LGBTQ+ community college students. Historically, centers that served queer and trans students began with a focus on White gay men. LGBTQ+ centers cannot use those same models and expect to serve community college students.

Colleges recommended LGBTQ+ efforts center transgender students' needs. Although this may be a minority in the community, the needs can often be very intense and there are many barriers to limit a student from succeeding. Final recommendations from the colleges surveyed focused on building collaborations and partnerships. LGBTQ+ groups attempting to start services should find allies in senior leadership roles and work collaboratively. If the local community has an LGBTQ+ center, it can also be beneficial to partner with local organizations for support and to be able to provide more robust services by outsourcing and collaborating.

The challenges will come, and the successes will follow. Creating services that are life-changing take time, resources, emotion, and persistence. The long-term results will come, and we must all start somewhere. Doing something small is still better than doing nothing. At times it can feel discouraging or hopeless, but we remind you that we may not end homophobia, transphobia, and injustice in one strategic planning cycle. However, we can move the needle towards being more equitable, justice focused, and ensure our students know they matter and we are here to support them.

5

Building Partnerships for Impact

> *We need strong, sincere, and impactful partnerships that builds strong and healthy communities for all!.*

Given the community place, location, and context, community colleges might be the only place where students have the actual in-person support to address some of their unique issues and to find a sense of belonging with others who are comfortable with LGBTQ+ people. Serving LGBTQ+ students from multiple generations, backgrounds, and situations, centers in community colleges need to be aware of the multitude of challenges that students might walk in the door with. Therefore, it is necessary to pay careful attention to identifying allies and accomplices at your college. It is important to remember that advocating on the behalf of a resource center and LGBTQ+ students, it is wise to build strong allies and partners that are within the institution and externally when meeting with boards, administrations and other governing bodies that hold the power to make decisions. Community college LGBTQ+ efforts should identify community resources in their towns, cities, or state and build partnerships.

In reflecting upon the development of LGBTQ+ community centers, support groups, and safe spaces, the fact that such organizations insisted on being created and survive and thrive in hostile social environments is a testament to the need and their purpose. LGBTQ+ centers in post-secondary institutions are similar to community peers and often have a very different set of clients, depending on their respected locations. In fact, how an institution and center define its roles and mission depend on the partnerships they will develop. LGBTQ+ centers, identity and cultural centers, on post-secondary campuses are different in various aspects, but it is clear that they both exist to service the LGBTQ+ populations. There is limited data that paints a picture of how such agencies support each other and even less when identifying exemplar examples of how post-secondary centers work with community agencies in a holistic way for their students.

What we do know is that many queer and trans students in community colleges face the same challenges as LGBTQ+ individuals in society but do so while also trying to obtain educational goals. Most centers and spaces for LGBTQ+ individuals have no choice but to address the effort to combat homelessness, end food insecurity, provide HIV testing, prevention, and education, and provide access to mental health resources for students and members of the LGBTQ+ community. Even though LGBTQ+ centers are situated within a community college context with a specific focus on students' success, the multiple personal issues one faces as a student must also be considered so that one progress is not curtailed in the academic progress.

Research articles document the importance of an institutional agent, advisor, or counselor as systemic collaborators with educational stakeholders—both inside and outside of educational organizations (American School Counselor Association [ASCA], 2012; Bryan & Henry, 2008, 2012; Epstein & Van Voorhis, 2010). According to a national counseling association, they underscore the importance of systemically working together through school, family, and community collaboration rather than creating silos of aloneness. By collaborating and utilizing shared resources organizations and communities can have a far greater chance of helping LGBTQ+ individuals (ASCA, 2012).

LGBTQ+ centers' purposes in community colleges are enhanced when they establish courageous allies and partnerships with community agencies to serve their students, faculty, and staff. The commitment to such partnerships benefits the entire institution when it strengthens its relationship with multiple agencies in the local community. Community colleges serve multiple roles in their local communities, and untapped potential exists for them to better understand how they can positively influence change for the citizens of the areas they serve.

The term *partnership* might be defined as the collaborations characterized by shared commitment of a diverse group of members to achieving a common goal (Johns et al., 2007). For community colleges, partnerships are becoming widely recognized by researchers as a means to increase the capacity of their communities to respond to their unique needs, especially the need for economic development (Johns et al., 2007; Lasker et al., 2001). Research literature recognizes that partnerships enable different people and organizations within a community to leverage and utilize their varying strengths and capabilities to address complex community and economic problems; however, they are also difficult to implement and sustain because they require relationships and structures that may not be typical (Austin, 2007; Lasker et al., 2001). However, for LGBTQ+ populations and networks, the individuals involved are more known and identified in smaller communities and cities. Individuals who are leaders of LGBTQ+ initiatives within the institution would most likely be involved in the community activities.

Partnerships differ in how they are organized and operate, yet there is a common thread among all of them. There is an understanding that individuals and organizations are being asked to do more with less and that no one entity can effectively accomplish objectives alone (Lasker et al., 2001). Again, working with little resources is where LGBTQ+ organizations have learned to partner together in amazing ways to serve individuals. There is no one "best way" to create and sustain partnerships between community colleges and community groups to serve students (Johns et al., 2007).

So, what does this mean for LGBTQ+ partnerships with the community? The queer and trans community encompass many different orientations and gender expressions. It is also commonly referred to as "the gay community," "the LGBT community," and even just "the community" when referred to among other members. LGBTQ+ centers and spaces are loosely defined by common goals, culture, subcultures, pride movements, and advocacy. Due to this loose configuration of individuals and goals in the queer and trans community, tensions exist that must also be addressed with regards to seeking partnerships. The literature is littered with issues within the LGBTQ+ community that deals with conflict regarding naming of centers, who should be included, what to focus on, and so on. Therefore, the attention on purpose and focus with partnerships should be taken up with great care and on emphasis to serve students.

In serving students, a center should think about who their students are and the conditions of their lives and how those impact a student's goals for their academic success, job training, or advance credentials. Advisors, faculty, and advocates for LGBTQ+ individuals need to be sensitive to both the social and mental health issues that are unique to this population. Often, the talent management or personnel within the community college may not have the expertise or the capacity to accommodate the needs of students, or worst yet—there may not be a center at all. Therefore, scanning the community for resources, individuals, or agencies to turn to for support. Coming resources and organizations creates a systemic ecological environment for the overall well-being of LGBTQ+ students, faculty, or staff. Regardless of the partnership, knowing what is needed by the college, staff, students, and faculty from the partnerships is essential to getting the outcomes wanted. One does not need to be too rigid in exploring partnerships and sharing resources. One should be open to developing stages with small wins before moving to larger ones; however, services and programming must remain at the center of the initiatives considering the needs of community college students.

For example, in various areas of the United States, LGBTQ+ individuals struggle with homelessness, mental health, and access to health care. Because community college students come from multiple generation and are not the "traditional age" of residential colleges, professionals will need to assess how to educate students with a variety of life issues including assistance with paying for schooling, food, health, mental issues, and basic life necessities. For example, according to the website Dosomething.org we find the following numbers about LGBTQ+ individuals on January 10, 2021:

- "42% of people who are LGBTQ+ report living in an unwelcoming environment.
- "80% of gay and lesbian youth report severe social isolation.
- "6 in 10 LGBTQ+ students report feeling unsafe at school because of their sexual orientation. You can encourage your classmates to accept LGBTQ+ students by promoting your views on social media.
- "90% of teens who are LGBTQ+ come out to their close friends.
- "While non-LGBTQ+ students struggle most with school classes, exams, and work, their LGBTQ+ peers say the biggest problem they face is unaccepting families.
- "As of January 2019, most transgender people are barred from serving in the military." ("11 Facts LGBT Life in America," n.d., nos. 1–4, 7, 9)

And even more disheartening data from the Funders for LGBTQ Issues website:

- "Transgender people face enormous health disparities, including staggering rates of HIV infection, lack of primary care (includ-

ing individualized, medically necessary transition-related healthcare), and high rates of attempted suicide.
- "Transgender people b ear the economic consequences of discrimination, including high rates of poverty and unemployment, discrimination in education, and homelessness. Trans people are more than twice as likely to live in extreme poverty (earning under $10,000 a year), with Latinx transgender people facing three-and-a-half times, and Black transgender people facing three times, the poverty rate of the general U.S. population.
- "Transgender people also experience frightening levels of physical violence, especially people participating in sex work and other informal or criminalized economies." ("Transgender Issues," n.d., para. 2–3)

The conditions of LGBTQ+ students living in society require community colleges to develop meaningful partnerships with multiple community agencies to serve the students. LGBTQ+ professionals on campus do not have a choice regarding their call to duties to serve vulnerable populations. One should keep in mind that organizations are made up of individuals who have networks inside and outside of the institution. And strong relationships among people—relationship-building—isn't a trait that comes naturally to everyone, especially when you have organizations like LGBTQ+ centers reaching out to heteronormative agencies. Emphasis on the importance and value of building trustworthy relationships of value must be firmly embedded with intent for any collaboration to work.

Regardless of the challenge, essential partners to consider are civic leaders, organizers, advocates, city and county agencies, and community members with the tools to navigate polarizing differences that might exist to form as allies for LGBTQ+ services. Such essential partners could always be used for engagement programs, community dialogues, public meetings, and workplace employment opportunities for students. The key to impactful partnerships is connection and relational with agreed upon purpose and financial commitments which take time to manage and maintain. Partnerships and collaborations have increased in popularity for solving the challenges of a rapidly changing world, but a lack of clear understanding as to why some succeed and some fail still exists (Barnett et al., 1999; Johns et al., 2007; Lasker et al., 2001). Partnerships are typically one-of-a-kind because they consist of unique people, values, priorities, and context (Barnett et al., 1999).

Another aspect that is essential for LGBTQ+ partnerships is to make sure that there are like values between the organizations, or at least there are mutual benefits of working together to enhance current organizational cultures and outcomes. Many city-focused LGBT centers are focused on older, White, and middle-class or higher LGBT populations. Despite the possible difficulties associated with their uniqueness, the potential benefits of partnership formation—to include leveraging resources, strengths, and capabilities—require that agencies, institutions, organizations, and individuals consider working together versus apart (Barnett et al., 1999; Johns et al., 2007; Lasker et al., 2001). One cannot expect to optimize a relationship with a strategic partner without understanding each other. This includes knowing the key individuals affecting the decisions, actions, and plans; the strengths and weaknesses; financial obligations; how services and resources might be shared; and the population served. For a community college with limited resources, especially LGBTQ+ centers, having partners to work with on funding issues such as grants and sources of funding is essential. At a minimum, community college LGBTQ+ center staff should know local community resources for referrals. Making sure that both organizations understand the terms of the partnerships with detailed expectations of each organization's commitment with boundaries helps with misunderstanding and assumptions.

The histories of advocacy, equal rights, and other legalistic issues that LGBTQ+ centers and spaces are entangled with due to the natural challenges, identities, voice, and public relations on multiple topics might also be explored for clarity. To avoid any confusion for students, faculty, and the public, both collaborative agencies should co-develop short, medium, and long-term objectives and goals. Such objectives and goals should be clear and shared throughout both organizations and with the public.

It is important to set regular meetings for updating each other in order to discuss challenges and opportunities of the partnership. Each partnership will be different based on varying agencies. LGBTQ+ centers should advocate to faculty, staff, and students to utilize their expertise when necessary to be included in research, practices, coursework, and professional development when necessary. Like most dynamic systems, partnerships will need constant attention to what is working and what is not; therefore, the ability to adjust and adapt to changing environments are necessary and should be understood by both partners.

Having annual reports, events, and opportunities to share with the general public and between organizations also helps advance the mission, goals, and objectives sought.

One should always remember that partnerships are not meant to be forever. Therefore, dissolving a partnership should be measured by the capacity developed within the LGBTQ+ center, the community, and the impactful implementation of programming.

Community College LGBTQ+ professionals can facilitate change at multiple levels by taking an active role in community and civic organizations. Working with other helping professionals increases the greater knowledge and awareness of ways to address the specific needs of LGBTQ+ students from the institutional and community perspectives. Remember such collaboration or partnership might include advocating for a change in policies, writing a grant for a joint cause, developing taskforce that includes both the town and college to address LGBTQ+ people that would also be systemic from health and safety to police brutality and homelessness. With regard to impact, the aim should always be to help individuals find ways to have a voice as students, professionals, and leaders in their institutions and communities and strengthen the ways in which queer and trans students and families are welcomed, included, engaged, and supported in the greater communities.

In summary, community colleges have such an important role in the activities of communities and in society. By having a collective consciousness to provide quality academics, training, and social services to students for developing and creating well rounded lives is more important than ever in the 21st century world. Although community colleges may not be able to provide for all the needs of students, institutions should build relevant and strong partnerships with those community agencies when possible to provide service to students and families. Due to the multiple issues of well-being that many LGBTQ+ individuals, especially transgender, face in society, having a resource, person, or place, that could make connections on the behalf of students in moments of crisis really matter. Partnership makes it possible for community colleges to create a repertoire of options to students that would not otherwise be available, and these options should be considered in the planning and sustaining future services provided. Equally important in building lasting effective partnerships is to remember to include practitioners who understand LGBTQ+ students' life challenges.

6

Practitioners' Voices

Introduction

As authors of this book, we wanted to include emerging research that is critical work for LGBTQ+ communities and social justice efforts. One researcher-practitioner we are privileged to hear from is Angel Gonzalez, who currently is a post-doctoral researcher at the University of Southern California. Their doctoral research focused on a sense of belonging for community college students, with a focus on queer and transgender students. Angel also previously served as an equity administrator at several community colleges. Sense of belonging is a key factor for academic success and there has been little research on sense of belonging for community colleges, so we asked Angel to contribute to this book. The following section is a contribution from Angel Gonzalez in August 2020 based off inquiring questions we provided.

DE COLORES: SENSE OF BELONGING FOR QTPOC COMMUNITY COLLEGE STUDENTS: A PRACTITIONER'S PERSPECTIVE BY DR. ANGEL GONZALEZ

All of us are put in boxes by our family, by our religion, by our society, our moment in history, even our own bodies. Some people have the courage to break free.

—Geena Rocero (2014)

It still infuriates me to think that in 2020, we still are discussing the need to exist in society broadly. I write to you from the lens of not just a researcher, a position curated by traditional hierarchical standards of education and knowledge production from a Eurocentric Westernized view, but a queer person, a *joto* (reclaimed derogatory term for faggot in Spanish, similar to queer in English), who has endured and continues to survive violence inflected on my body in a variety of structures. As someone who has witnessed this violence replicated and perpetuated to my queer and trans* siblings within the work I do, my purpose has become the need to advocate for recognition, inclusivity, and existence in these spaces within higher education. For about 7 years now, I have worked at various institutional types to include: large public, small private, liberal arts, religiously affiliated, and community colleges. Within these colleges and universities, I have also worked across various functional/service areas such as residential life, student life, academic services, student services, diversity, equity and inclusion initiatives, student code of conduct, and many more. I have found that within these curated structures, student experiences are compartmentalized and attempted to be served in silos versus holistically and through an intersectional manner. I have seen this time and time again.

More noticeably during my time at community colleges, I saw the ways in which inadequate access to funding and services manifested into inequitable outcomes for students. My focus on community colleges is twofold. On a personal note, I have two sisters who are currently at a community college navigating the bureaucratic system to transfer. For one, community college provided the flexibility and access to attend at her own pace due to her being a full-time mother, wife, daughter, sister, and student. For another, community college allows her the ability to explore career paths, manage mental health needs, and also support family obligations of being the youngest Latina daughter. Yet, on the back end as an educator, I hear from them the gaps that exist for their support, and the labyrinth of policies and practices. This informed the switch to position myself as an educator within the community college system to try and provide students, the best

I can, what my sisters shared they were missing. Secondly, similarly to my sisters, there are so many other students with minoritized backgrounds at community colleges trying to navigate the best they can—often without adequate support.

Community College Landscape

According to National Center for Education Statistics (NCES, 2018), about 38% of all undergraduates were enrolled in community college. This means that close to half of all undergraduate students are enrolled at community colleges. With this in mind, the majority of students enrolled at community colleges are those from minoritized backgrounds. I used minoritized instead of "minority" as conceptual framing to signify that persons are not born into a minority status but are made subordinate, oppressed through supremacist structures by U.S. social institutions (Gillborn, 2015; Harper, 2012). An example of this is the way in which minoritized students make the largest population within community colleges, yet community colleges broadly are underfunded in comparison to their 4-year counterparts with the expectation to serve a far more diverse student demographic with less services. Community colleges within the landscape of higher education are becoming first choice educational paths for students' post-secondary journeys now more than ever. This is especially true for students from minoritized backgrounds. Community colleges offer proximity to home, are open access, associated with lower cost, and offer an array of programs from transfer pathways to certificate short-term workforce training. This combination attracts students who might be first generation (the first in their families to attend college), who are students of color given the role collectivism in communities of color play, and with that, the potential for immediate financial contribution to their family.

In the latest enrollment report from the American Association of Community Colleges, (AACC, n.d.), enrollment trends noted that the percentage of White students decreased by 13.8% from a high of 60% in 2001 to 46.2% in 2017. I want to note too that "White" as a demographic category can be problematic as currently race and ethnicity are constructs not often differentiated or dissected separately and people who might be from minoritized identities might also identify as White (i.e., Latinx/a/o, Hispanic, Arabic, Middle Eastern people). Furthermore, when we think about the percentage of students of color at community colleges, by 2017 Latinx/a/o students made up nearly a quarter (24.9%) of community college enrollments, Black students comprised only 12.7%, Asian Pacific Islander 6.3%, and with the least proportion in enrollments were Native American at 1.0% (AACC, n.d.). Furthermore, it is important to note that even though minoritized students represent most of the student enrollments at community colleges, only 7% attain a bachelor's degree within 10 years (AACC, n.d.). As we consider the ability to disaggregate data amongst various demographic groups, gender metrics overwhelmingly remain binary, with 56.3% female and 42.7% male enrollments. I would love to write about the percentage number of the amount of lesbian, gay, bisexual, transgender, queer, and more (LGBTQ+) students enrolled at community colleges in the nation, but woefully I still cannot. It is here where my research, purpose, and aim are situated to interrogate the structures and systems that influence the conditions, experiences, and outcomes of LGBTQ+ students at community colleges.

From the Past to the Present

I shared my positionality as it pertains to my focus on community colleges, I offer you the same in regard to LGBTQ+ students and queer and transgender students of color (QTSOC). As a queer Latinx person who is genderfluid expressive and cis male, I navigate my body at the opposition of institutions that do not know what to do with me. This has always been the case. This too has been the connecting piece for the LGBTQ+ students and queer and trans students of color (QTSOC) I have served as a practitioner at community colleges. This has made me the go-to for LGBTQ+ matters on campus, the advisor to the PRIDE organization, the Ally Trainer, and the list continues on top of my actual job duties. Have I been tired? Yes. Has it been worth it? Yes, it has—for all the QTSOC and LGBTQ+ students who get to have their first supervisor that looks like them, that can talk about pop culture to them, that can share herstory of our ancestors Marsha P. Johnson and Sylvia Rivera, that can at a basic level ask for their pronouns and self-chosen name. It was worth it for the time we hosted the first ever queer prom and a colleague who was a classified custodian staff member in their mid-40s—who is an openly transgender woman—tell me, "Thank you so much for doing this. I have never felt so seen. I did not get to go to prom in high school as myself, just thank you." This is why I believe in the work that I do and the work so many of us are doing in order to exist and survive in spaces that tell us otherwise.

Although strides have been made to create inclusive campuses, community colleges remain far from reaching their potential in supporting LGBTQ+ people. In 1991, Judith Baker "shattered the silence" demanding that gay and lesbian students be included across the fabric of junior and community colleges in a way that disrupted the heterosexism on campuses. Baker called upon us in higher education to adopt nondiscrimination policies, curriculum that was inclusive of LGBTQ+ people, and to increase the amount of LGBTQ+ leaders across institutions (Baker, 1991). And have we answered this call? No. The reality is that we have not made the necessary and crucial policy-supported changes to mobilize higher education broadly—and community colleges in specific—to better support LGBTQ+ students.

In 2012, Steven Leider provided us a 20-year review of LGBTQ+ people at community colleges. The literature review covered once again brought front and center Baker's original argument of the need for community colleges to be inclusive of their LGBTQ+ students. Leider positioned that a basic understanding of LGBTQ+ students was needed to inform policies and practices, to identify and address barriers prohibiting positive outcomes, and to implement and sustain systemic change (Leider, 2012). Now, almost a decade later, we still have yet to make waves towards achieving this. Current campus climate at community colleges for LGBTQ+ students continue to remain hostile given the lack of visibility, validation, and safety across institutions (Garvey et al., 2015; Rankin, 2005; Rankin et al., 2010; Renn & Patton, 2010). There are many factors that contribute to campus climate (Hurtado, 1994; Garvey et al., 2015; Garvey & Rankin, 2015) and a sense of belonging (Strayhorn, 2012, 2018; Zamani-Gallaher & Choudhuri, 2011) for community college students. Often homophobia, transphobia, and cisheterogenderism institutionally embedded that preferences heterosexism, are the prominent factors influencing campus climates for LGBTQ+ community college students. These hostile campuses—or more recently designated "traditionally heterogendered institutions" (THI; Preston & Hoffman, 2015)—are not new spaces to navigate for LGBTQ+ community college students. Franklin's (1998) study was key in quantifying in the academy the rampant violence against LGBTQ+ community college students. She administered a survey to 500 cisgender heterosexual students and the results yielded that half, 250, of the respondents were cishetero men who admitted to being perpetrators of violence and harassment towards LGBTQ+ students (Franklin, 1998). According to Franklin (1998), out of all acts of violence rooted in homophobia, 72% were done in paring, meaning with another cishetero person (Ivory, 2012). Infuriating, and sadly, this is the reality today. Violence and hate fueled by homophobia, transphobia, and cisheterogenderism permeate the policies and practices of institutions, causing without a doubt an impact on LGBTQ+ community college students' mental health and sense of belonging.

Now let's consider the aforementioned through an intersectional lens. Intersectionality as a conceptual framing was coined in academia by Kimberly Crenshaw (1989), who centered the narratives of Black woman noting their dual oppression experienced due to their gender (patriarchy) and their race (racism). She explained how "Black woman" is not an additive identity of "Black" plus "woman," but rather a full one of being a Black woman in any setting at any given time (Crenshaw, 1989). Crenshaw offers us this tool as a way to examine oppressive structures that subordinate a certain group through the compounding oppression of social constructs who have historically had power. Therefore, when we consider LGBTQ+ students of color, or QTSOC, they exist and navigate structures associated with their LGBTQ+ identities (cisheterogenderism) and race (racism). Scholarship on the impact of living at the intersections of these identities have been done by many scholars, with a primary focus on 4-year institutions. Time and time again the results are the same—the lack of support and validating agents (Rendon, 1994), hostile campus climates (Garvey, 2015; Garvey et al., 2015; Gortmaker & Brown, 2006), and lack of services and resources impact sense of belonging (Duran, 2019; Strayhorn, 2012, 2019).

The various pieces highlighted before as it pertains to the visibility, campus climate, and ultimately identity development of LGBTQ+ community college students are all intertwined with the need to ensure students have a sense of belonging. Students' sense of belonging has been a phenomenon studied by many scholars. At a basic level, this relates to students' own sense of feeling like they are welcomed in their campus community. Strayhorn (2012, 2019) considered that sense of belonging as the students' perceived social support that manifests through a feeling of connectedness to the college environment and the experience of mattering to the campus community. These factors are exacerbated at community colleges. Because community colleges tend to be commuter campuses, students with minoritized identities, in this case QTSOC, have the pressure of navigating their outness—meaning their identity saliency and development (Cass, 1984; D'Augelli, 1991; Fassinger, 1991; Garvey & Rankin, 2015)—both at home and on campus. The dual distress experienced by QTSOC due to their intersecting identities impacts academic performance, engagement on campus, and student success (Duran, 2019; González & Cataño, 2020; Pascarella & Terenzini, 2005). As community college leaders, we need to consider the ways in which we uphold traditionally heterogendered institutions causing harm and violence to our queer and trans* students of color and LGBTQ+ students.

Current Research

In order to aid the void of literature around queer and trans* students of color at community colleges and broadly LGBTQ+ community college scholarship (Ivory, 2012), my research agenda centers LGBTQ+ community college students and professionals through intersectionality, critical queer epistemologies, and feminist thought praxis. Currently, I am working on multiple research projects both qualitative and quantitative in nature. One prominent study I'm working on with Dr. Wendy Bracken at San Diego State University (SDSU) examines the role images that depict LGBTQ+ representation play on LGBTQ+ community college students' sense of belonging. Quantitative research has demonstrated a correlation between racially salient images and positive outcomes for student of color (Bracken & Wood, 2019). Similarly, we expand and explore this phenomenon of images in validating LGBTQ+ students. As noted above, campus climate research as it pertains to LGBTQ+ community college students are a growing strand of literature categorized into three areas: visibility, campus climate, and identity development and experiences (Renn, 2010). I owe the scholars that I cited a great deal of acknowledgment since their research and writing has provided visibility and a place for me to being exploring sense of belonging for LGBTQ+ community college students. I focus on the conditions, experiences, and outcomes for queer and trans* people at community colleges while utilizing various research methods to help gather their voices, elevate their presence, and demand recognition of existence.

This is an ongoing study where we have conducted interviews through a queer phenomenology perspective (Ahmed, 2006a). Traditionally, phenomenological studies have explored the meaning making of a participants' lived experience to develop an overview of an experience—a phenomenon (Moustakas, 1994). However, queer phenomenology is not just as a description of the phenomenon but focuses on dissecting texts, formation, and dismantling of constructs of dominant society taking into consideration historical structures, exclusionary societal underpinnings of queer people, and the reasons these exists in the first place (Ahmed, 2006b). We continue to collect data and analyze current findings; however, the following emerging themes have been identified: (a) for students by students, LGBTQ+ clubs as primary support; and (b) images such as meaningful logos and symbols as signs of safety. As this study continues to shape, we must acknowledge that students are taking the burden of creating inclusive spaces for themselves—this on top of their academic endeavors, paired with identity distress associated with hostile campus climates.

Where Do We Go, What Do We Do?

Even after 2 decades since the call to action to address the visibility, safety, and belonging of LGBTQ+ community college students, nothing has changed at a systemic level. Initiatives remain at the emotional labor, burden, and cost of the students we should be trying to serve and support. Very minimal institutionalized supports exist for LGTBQ+ community college students. Primary is the inherently transphobic and homophobic data collecting mechanisms that perpetuate erasure, promote invisibility, and ultimately remove LGBTQ+ students from the material reality of access to higher education. Data metrics still lack a critical lens that pushes the opportunity to capture the collective estimate of who are our LGBTQ+ community college students. Therefore, the tiresome narrative of, "We don't know who these students are," continues, the lack of financial priority remains, and LGBTQ+ community college students continue to be left at the margins.

A starting point that I echo from my past scholar predecessors is to collect data on our students! College application portals, financial aid processes, and demographics questionnaires at every level should not be gender binary nor heteronormative. We cannot institutionalize support for LGBTQ+ students if they do not exist in the most basic of ways—enrollment and demographics. If community colleges will continue to pride itself in their open access to higher education, we must be equitable in our approach to who we say we serve. I ask for institutional leaders at every level to question their current practices. Where can you have immediate influence and impact? As a chancellor of a multi community college district, can you propose a resolution to your board of trustees to consider adding an LGBTQ+ identifier in your application? As a director of financial aid, can you add LGBTQ+ metrics to note the financial impact and aid being distributed or not for LGBTQ+ students? As a dean for academic services who works with faculty, can you revise and ensure curriculum that is inclusive of LGBTQ+ identities? We are at a crux in higher education where community colleges are positioned in a place to transform the lives of our students, are we willing to answer to that call and allow the visibility and existence of LGBTQ+ students and professionals by adding at a basic level an opportunity to claim self? We should not have to debate students' opportunity to be themselves in a world that tells them they do not belong. In the current socio-political landscape where hate is rampant, we should not be another barrier that prevents from love. If we say and believe that community college are access points for opportunity and change, then we must change and actually be that for all students. In this case; namely, for queer and trans students.

As authors of this book, we wanted to highlight experts doing critical work for LGBTQ+ communities and social justice efforts. There are authors, educators, activists, and practitioners who have insights and perspectives that we can all learn from. One practitioner we are privileged to hear from is Dr. Raja Bhattar, who currently serves as a social justice consultant, author, educator, speaker, and community college faculty member. Dr. Bhattar has led LGBT centers and other equity focused efforts at the University of California–Los Angeles and the University of Chicago; they have also consulted for numerous community colleges. The following section is a contribution from Dr. Raja Bhattar (July, 2020).

SUPPORTING COMMUNITY COLLEGE STUDENTS AT THE INTERSECTIONS: A PRACTITIONER'S PERSPECTIVE BY DR. RAJA GOPAL BHATTAR

> *Your lives matter. Your voices matter. Your stories matter.*
> —Laverne Cox (2016)

> *We are not what other people say we are. We are who we know ourselves to be, and we are what we love. That's okay.*
> —Laverne Cox (2016)

Lesbian, gay, bisexual, transgender, queer/questioning (LGBTQ) students on community college campuses are more diverse and visible than ever before. In my role as the director of UCLA's LGBTQ Campus Resource Center (the Center), I got to work with incredible transfer students coming from various community colleges and experiences from across the country. Many of these students spoke about the critical gap in services and programs to support LGBTQ students at the community college level. While each student loved their community college education, they noted the absence of an LGBTQ-centered program/office as a barrier to personal development and sense of belonging on campus. Access to social media, community activism, and the current state of politics, students arriving on campus today demand higher levels of attention to identity and intersectionality topics. Even colleges with multicultural or diversity offices often lack competency and resources to adequately support LGBTQ students—especially students at the intersection of race and/or disability. Though students may only spend a few years on campus, for many it is the first time they get to engage in self-exploration at academic and personal levels.

Some potential barriers to supporting intersectional LGBTQ identity at the community college level are:

- *Absence of or under-resourced identity centers*: Often these centers are overstretched and lack capacity to support the breadth of diverse identities within the student body.
- *College leadership*: While higher education leaders tout the importance of diversity, community college leaders may not fully understand or embrace a true intersectional understanding of identity and the necessity of identity-based resources for student success.
- *Lack of research*: Community college students constitute a significant portion of all college students in the United States, yet research on community college students and social identity development is lacking.

These are significant systemic barriers, but with strategic action and allocation of resources, community college campuses can meet the developmental needs of their students and transform their experiences. As the first director of color of the Center, I was often challenged when bringing up concepts of intersectionality, such as race, socioeconomic class, (dis)ability, international student status, and faith. I had some colleagues and students ask, "Shouldn't you just focus on gay stuff? Why do you always have to talk about race or ability? Why do you make everything so complicated?" My response was often a version of: "I can't talk about sexuality or gender without contextualizing them within a holistic sense of identity." Those of us who hold intersectional identities live in this messiness every moment. Our work must be intersectional to be transformative. While my role focused on directly addressing gender and sexuality topics on campus, my framework is grounded in social justice and intersectional understanding of identity.

Further, when I walk into a room, my skin color and gender expression are often most obvious to others. My understanding of queerness is influenced by my racialization and other identities such as spirituality, class, immigration status, and more. The students coming to campus today have more access and awareness of these various elements of identity than ever before. While race is dominant in our discussions of diversity and inclusion, it cannot exist without a holistic approach to our students' growth. Developing silo-ed identity spaces contributes to a false expression of oppression Olympics and denies an appreciation for the messiness of human identity. In a groundbreaking article on Black lesbian women, scholar Lisa Bowleg (2008) notes that identifying as Black, lesbian, or woman is not the same as identifying as a Black lesbian woman. Removing the commas is an essential act of liberation. We are not simply the sum of our various layers of identity; we are the fusion of these elements in constant evolution.

In my most recent campus role, I oversaw an inclusion office with three specific offices dedicated to race, sexuality and gender, and first-generation and undocumented student status. While there are various perspectives comparing the effectiveness of individual identity services (i.e., LGBTQ center) versus all-encompassing offices (i.e., diversity center), a hybrid model is best to meet the intersectional needs of LGBTQ community college students today. For students comfortable enough and far along in their identity development to enter an LGBTQ center, the space can be a powerful experience for growth and community building. Indeed, I remember many transfer students walking in on admitted students' day itching to get involved and expressing struggles with a lack of such spaces on their community college campuses. Yet for others who need more indirect paths, we needed to build relationships and a sense of shared purpose with other identity offices, especially those supporting transfer students.

Intersectionality, in practice, requires intentionality, expertise, and collaboration. Beyond professing inclusion, campuses committed to these students must assess accessibility of current resources along with a deep reflection on why developing intersectional frameworks are critical to student development and success. Though LGBTQ communities are represented as a single identity, they encompass an incredible diversity of sexualities and gender identities/expressions. Recognizing such breadth can help diminish stereotyping and unintentional exclusion of particular identities within the LGBTQ umbrella. This process only gets more important and difficult when we understand how other aspects of identity (i.e., race, ability, and immigration) impact how the campus student population interacts with the LGBTQ office. Developing a keen understanding of the campus demographics the surrounding community will be important to demonstrate intentionality and mitigate unintentional impact.

While intentionality is helpful, expertise and relevant knowledge needs to be demonstrated by regular and robust training for faculty and staff on concepts of intersectionality, identity, and campus climate. Developing student support offices with a strong foundation in the theories and practices of intersectional identity development can ensure these offices offer innovative programs and engagement opportunities for students. Moreover, establishing interdisciplinary academic programs such as ethnic studies and gender and sexuality studies with tenured faculty focused on the intersections of identities, is essential for supporting students. Academic faculty researching intersectionality and identity along with opportunities for student research can enhance student knowledge and engagement across campus units.

Fostering a culture of collaboration across units, especially units supporting specific identities (i.e., disability services, international student programs, etc.), will result in a cohesive experience for students. As educators, we have a responsibility to build relationships across campus to foster a culture of belonging and for students because of, not in spite of, their intersectional identities (Strayhorn, 2019). Developing a campus of colleagues who are clear about their own work and how and when to connect with other offices, reduces program duplication and sense of territoriality.

As I conclude, I will share some specific strategies to support LGBTQ students and all their intersections on your college:

- Ensure representation of intersectional LGBTQ identities in marketing and campus art.
- Create programs and ensure student leadership funding is earmarked to highlight and support queer and trans people of color (QTPOC) communities.
- Update non-discrimination statements to include intersections of identities.
- Regularly assess campus forms and policies to enhance inclusion.
- Engage students in making policy and resource allocation decisions.
- Have a keen understanding of student demographics and intersectionality identity needs.
- Allocate funding to ensure multiple staff positions within identity centers.
- Develop hiring and assessment processes to increase diversity and expertise in multiple areas of the college.
- Establish a campus intersectionality committee to gather expertise and enhance campus advocacy.
- Partner with local 4-year institutions to share resources and build cohesive transitions for transfer students.
- Partnering with community organizations will also enhance critical mass for intersectional identities.
- Develop a robust database of local, national, and international organizations/resources.

While this list is in no way comprehensive, these strategies offer individual, interpersonal, and structural level interventions to enhance intersectional sense of belonging, inclusion, and identity development on campus (Bhattar, 2019; Crenshaw, 1991; Martinez & Munsch, 2019).

As authors of this book, we recognize that we do not have all the answers or expertise. However, we do know there are other powerful educators doing meaningful work across the country. One practitioner we are privileged to hear from is Dr. Claudia Mercado, who currently is the interim vice president of the Office of Diversity, Equity, and Inclusion at Harper College in Palatine, Illinois. Dr. Mercado's role as a chief diversity officer includes employee support in addition to student and community advocacy. We asked Dr. Mercado to share insights and promising practices on how a community college could best support LGBTQ+ employees. The following section is a contribution from Dr. Claudia Mercado from July 2020.

SUPPORTING LGBTQ+ EMPLOYEES IN THE COMMUNITY COLLEGE: A PRACTITIONER'S PERSPECTIVE BY DR. CLAUDIA MERCADO

> *Be yourself, the world will adjust.*
> —Manabi Bandyopadhyay (2016)

LGBTQA+ employees at community colleges need the support and recognition from their college more than one might think. It can be difficult to work with majority cisgender and heterosexual colleagues in environments that still separate by sex and gender in rituals, spaces, and policies. There are many things, small and large, that can contribute to a positive environment. Based on my own experiences as a chief diversity officer (CDO) and as a member of the LGBTQ+ community, I would like to provide three promising practices.

One, LGBTQ+ employees need to have visible counter spaces throughout the college. Counter spaces provide safe spaces that simultaneously validate and critique one's interconnected self and group identity that would enable radical growth (Keels, 2019). While counter spaces provide space for students who come from oppressed and marginalized populations to feel validated and appreciated for their stories, this can also occur for community college employees. Counter spaces allow for LGBTQ+ employees to unpack other challenges/questions they have. These counter spaces can be through physical structures like a cultural center or identity specific community space that is designed not only for students but also employees from historically marginalized communities. Cultural centers can be designed for both/either students and employees, which often undergo similar challenges to addressing identity, culture awareness, and provide culturally responsive imagery.

In addition to a culture center, gender neutral bathrooms found in each physical building are important for transgender and non-binary employees. Whether they are single stalled or multiple stalled, it is important for LGBTQ+ employees to find a space they can feel comfortable in without worrying about their gender identity or expression. As a gender queer employee, I want to enter whatever bathroom without worrying about someone calling me sir or being told I entered the wrong bathroom. Something as simple as a bathroom can make a significant impact on how one feels about their workplace.

A last counter space is to provide an LGBTQ+ employee resource group (ERG). ERGs are employee recognized groups that center on employee identities such as race, ability, or sexuality. ERGs help provide an inclusive workplace which increases employee engagement, commonalities across divisions, and intersections across an employee's identities (Diversity Best Practices, 2018). ERGs can be coordinated with human resources and an office of DEI—similar to how student organizations are structured. The community college can provide financial support; organized structure; and institutional support for events, functions, etc.

A second-best practice is to count your employees. Like the census, it is important to count your people. LGBTQ+ employees want to be included in employee data points, scorecards, and dashboards, but are often excluded in those various data sets. As a CDO, the common data set for employees is race and gender. As a person of color, my race and gender are important, but they are no more important to me than my sexual orientation and gender expression. The intersectionality of our identities each matter and make us who we are. It can appear that when a college is only counting a portion of you in their data collection and reporting, a salient identity isn't relevant.

Community colleges often do not have the resources to collect additional data from employees without concern of impacting an employee's privacy. Collaborative efforts between human resources, institutional research, and an office of diversity, equity, and inclusion (DEI) can help develop appropriate questions, data storage, and reportable metrics that assist the community college in understanding the gender identity, gender expression, and sexuality of its employees. Being counted increases a sense of belonging, which is vitally important for employees of marginalized groups. Having data on LGBTQ+ employees will allow the college to analyze representation, hiring patterns, retention issues, and promotional pathways. If a college wants bonus points, they will go beyond just counting and also inquire to the experiences and satisfaction of LGBTQ+ employees.

Lastly, it's critically important to support and advocate for your LGBTQ+ employees. I have sat in cabinet meetings when we discussed whether we should make a statement when there was a national issue impacting LGBTQ+ community. Sometimes there is reason to make a statement and other times college leadership passes on crafting those important words of support. As a senior administrator, I understand we sometimes do not make statements because of the fear that if we acknowledge one group, we must do the same for each group. I disagree with this ideology. Whether the messages are sent to the ERG directly, internally to employees, posted on social media, the impact is still significant. LGBTQ+ employees want to know their community college is supporting them through local and national issues which allows them to remain productive and happier employees.

Overall, there is no single approach to supporting LGBTQ+ employees in community colleges. The opportunities depend on the community climate, the college's history, and its leadership. As in any systematic changes, leadership must support the needs of all its diverse populations. In equity work, the community college must learn what its LGBTQ+ employees need and provide the adequate and necessary support. The building of learning environments with reciprocal respect and support for LGBTQ+ employees is always a great place to start.

7

Students' Voices

> *Self-definition and self-determination are about the many varied decisions that we make to compose and journey toward ourselves... It's OK if your personal definition is in a constant state of flux as you navigate the world.*
>
> —Janet Mock (2014)

It is critical to us as authors to include the voices that this book is all about, our students. We are honored to feature several powerful narratives from powerful activists, poets, peer educators, and leaders. The stories presented in this next section are the experiences of a broad range of queer and trans community college students. These were current students or those who recently graduated or left a community college. They provide in brilliant detail the individual struggles and triumphs of our diverse student community. Each writer explores their identity and their experience through the intersecting identities that each hold. We chose to very minimally edit and to keep the students' words and format in their chosen words. These narratives are their authentic voice and what they chose to share to community college faculty, staff, administrators, and leaders.

Note: *In order to best prepare our readers, this chapter includes mention of domestic violence.*

CONSIDERING A STUDENT VOICE: "YOU KNOW WHAT THEY SAY ABOUT COLLEGE" BY ELAINE NICHOLSON

There's a joke that I heard a lot growing up about how college was a place where people, especially young women, "found" themselves and came out as gay. I thought it was a ridiculous stereotype and couldn't believe that it was something that got repeated on a regular basis.

Then I went to college, found myself, and came out as queer.

Before college, I stumbled my way through adolescence, trying to navigate other obstacles before I could even consider whether there was a closet for me to come out of despite all the evidence that I was definitely at least a little gay. The problem was that I also had to deal with being mentally ill from a young age, I came from a struggling working-class family, and I stopped caring about my education once I found out a college fund wasn't something families like mine had access to. I was confused, bordered on out of control, and didn't know where I fit in. I tried finding myself in a lot of places. I made questionable friends, nearly failed out of high school, started consuming a lot of LGBTQ+ media (the one positive move I made), and kissed anyone at parties regardless of gender because I thought that was just what you *did* in high school. At sixteen, I started dating a 19-year-old guy and fell in love the way all teenagers do; in under a week with the wrong person. I thought I had found someone I fit with. I didn't understand that a lot of his behaviors were huge red flags, because I was still a kid. By the time we had been together for 6 months, I thought I was going to marry him one day and he had started to hit me when he was angry. It continued for 4 years, getting worse and worse until I couldn't recognize myself anymore.

Having an already inconsistent sense of self coupled with the trauma of ongoing abuse meant that when I entered college at 19 with the intention of majoring in geology, I couldn't really tell you who I was at that time. Even now, I think back and can only remember being very lost. I was engaged and more alone than I had ever been in my entire life. By the time I was able to leave my abuser I was 20, and I had changed my major to psychology in an effort to try to help other people and maybe figure myself out. I reconnected with a friend from junior high school named Michael during a history class we took together. One day, he asked if I wanted to go with him to a GSA meeting. Without hesitation, I said, "Yes."

I introduced myself at my first GSA meeting as: "Elaine, straight ally, I guess." As time went on, I started to care more and more about the issues and history that were discussed in that room every week. I was asked to lead more than one discussion, especially regarding LGBTQ+ history and media because I had knowledge of both. I found people that liked the same things I liked, cared about the same social issues I cared about, and didn't think I was weird for knowing so much about things like LGBTQ+ history. In fact, it was a positive trait in that meeting room. We had events for the club and had *fun*, enjoying being around other people who loved the community and feeling like there was a shared culture. They were extremely kind when, at 21 (now a theater major), I said that I might actually be open to loving people of any gender. The next year, I was 22, a film major, and I was pretty sure I was "not entirely straight, actually." Bless everyone, they didn't bat an eye or say, "We know. *Everyone* knows." They gave me the space to talk about it and didn't pass judgement as I kept trying to figure out where I fit.

Then, right as I was starting to look around with new, hopeful little gay eyes, I dropped out of school. I couldn't pay for it; my parents couldn't pay for it. I was adrift and working on independent movies with a co-worker and hoping for *something* to happen. I signed on as a production assistant for an LGBTQ+ web series, and I was suddenly reconnected with the community. Shortly thereafter, I punched my way out of the closet, furious with myself for having gotten stuck there in the first place. With the understanding that I learned from the rest of my community, I began to accept parts of myself as they were and learned to cope with parts that needed healing. Through all of this, the GSA members I was still in contact with offered support and love, as if I had never left that meeting room.

When I went back to college in 2018, I was 28, a history major, and I was queer (or the nebulous "mostly gay"). During that first semester back, I was introduced to the faculty advisor for the newly revived GSA, and I was encouraged to join in the fall. I did, and once I overcame my initial shyness, it felt like I had come back to a place I had been missing that had been a much bigger part of me than I had ever realized. Coming back into that space, I felt like I was coming in with the confidence in my identity that I had seen in others when I first joined the club. I was now someone who had more or less settled into themselves and was comfortable making jokes about and references to my own experiences. I could look everyone in the eye and say, "Hi, I'm Elaine. I'm queer." I felt comfortable supporting people in that space the way that I had once desperately needed that same support.

Community college gave me the space to figure out who I was. I started community college in 2009 as a heterosexual, cis geology major who wanted to put together dinosaur bones in museum basements. I transferred in 2020 to a really good university as a queer, mostly gay historian who's figuring out their gender identity but doing fine. In those 11 years, I went through a journey of self-discovery and found myself *because* of financial hardship, trauma, and a community that I didn't realize was waiting for me. I sometimes think that I am a different person than when I entered college, but the reality is that I just found the person who had been too afraid and too conflicted and yanked them out into the world.

CONSIDERING A STUDENT VOICE: "FRONTERIZO" BY CESAR VIZCAINO

Include everyone, no matter their gender, orientation, race, or religion. We are all human beings and we are part of society.
—Lea T

Ever since I came out, my life went in an abundant amount of directions, I couldn't possibly ponder to say what was next, where time had stopped and when days started fading into hours, and then into minutes, seconds, and milliseconds. Sometimes I ask myself if I would start all over again whenever my heart stops, what a pain. Perhaps, as the human body obsesses over adrenaline, I would do everything all over again just to see and feel how the days faded into hours, minutes, seconds, and milliseconds.

As a bisexual male, I've dealt with numerous hardships that have put me in situations so overwhelming I've been left shattered and demoralized. Homelessness, discrimination, hatred, abuse, accusations, constant judgment, questioning as to whether or not it was right to love another male or if it was just a contradiction of the heart and impulses of the flesh; as I was told many times by parental and ecclesiastical figures; what an ad-hominem. Growing up as *fronterizo* (a person who lives on a national border), life moved in a different way than for most people. As a Mexican American *fronterizo* and native to the San Diego/Tijuana community, I've experienced situations that have tested my knowledge and intelligence regarding concepts of racial equity, diversity, minorities, border issues, educational issues, gender issues, and inequality. Growing up in Mexico, while also studying in the United States was not an easy task, yet I was resilient enough to succeed and move forward. I feel the hardest thing in an already conflicting environment was mustering the personal strength and will to come out and be proud of who I am. For the longest time I felt confused, and as my teenage and adult years progressed, my situation got worse before it got better.

I felt alone. I had no support. My thoughts were not becoming clearer. I was changing into something I did not understand but knew it was the right thing, because out of all the judgment, hatred, and discrimination towards me, I was at ease, because I knew it was just the typical existential hardships I had to endure to find myself and my purpose.

When I started college in the states, I was a young man that thought he knew so much, yet it was the opposite. I knew nothing. I had seen so little of what was required to bestow upon integrity, to construct a good moral foundation. At Southwestern College I had the opportunity to meet wise mentors and incredible role models that granted me the tools to become outspoken towards inequities and push for inclusivity in my community. For the first time I felt someone was there, listening, caring, and paying attention. I never thought I would get to where I am now. The LGBTQIA services at my college gave me so much support, so much love, and best of all their attention. I felt someone cared about me. They were able to provide me with a new job when resources were scarce, a home when I had no shelter, food when I was starving, and love to move forward.

Working for the college gave me the opportunity to channel all my energy in equitable and just change for the students, the community, and for myself. I created incredible friendships and was even lucky enough to find love. The people I met and those relationships will be with me in my future life and endeavors. I came from sleeping in the streets, being homeless, and having nothing, to graduating from my college, having been involved in campus politics and equity issues, as well as having the opportunity to work with a diverse community, and best of all, I had found myself and my purpose. As a Mexican American, *fronterizo*, person of color, first-generation immigrant, and part of the LGBT+ community, I wouldn't have imagined I would've made it this far. Moreover, I wish I could say that what follows is going to be easier, that success is eminent, and life will go on happily ever after. But alas, we know that is not the case. Life doesn't get easier, you only get stronger.

Through my journey I learned even the most impoverished can make a difference and achieve the impossible. Having been an advocate for students and my community I believe everyone can make a difference. Those who were previously incarcerated can make a change. A disability is just the ability to appreciate the world from a better perspective. A different lover is not a sin and every gender deserves equal treatment. We should be free to live our cultures openly and without demonization. Latino people, Black people, Asian people, Pacific Islander people, White people, and people of every culture of humanity can interrupt evil and strive for a better future for us, for our children, and the generations yet to come.

CONSIDERING A STUDENT VOICE: "RESTORING OUR COMMUNITIES" BY ALEJANDRA LANDIN

My silences had not protected me. Your silence will not protect you.
—Audre Lorde (*The Cancer Journals*)

While I was doing time, I found myself wondering why it would be worth it for me to go back to school. I made up my mind that school would be the place where I would build my own life compass that would not lead me astray, no matter what the map ahead looked like. When I first decided to go to school, distance learning was the vital bridge that allowed me to get on board the college path. Thanks to having a library branch within walking distance of the halfway house where I initially had to reside, I was able to leverage public library computer resources to take online classes. Unfortunately, in order to be permitted time to visit that library and study, I had to be "in the closet" about it. The for-profit (traded on the New York Stock Exchange as GEO) halfway house I had to reside in was only interested in residents getting jobs so it could collect 25% of our gross earnings, and to that end, had nuanced methods of dissuading residents by creating artificial barriers through programmatic rules sanctioned by the Federal Bureau of Prisons. This turned my desire to educate and better myself into a fugitive act. Luckily, my gumption prevailed, and I was able to leverage my local public library branch as my oasis and launchpad. I have the deepest gratitude and utmost respect for the Oakland Public Library staff that treated me with care, dignity, and exemplary service.

Had it not been for online classes, and access to computers at the library, I don't know that I would have tried college because of the social anxiety I had being around too many people and the overstimulation I experienced post-release. I also experienced intense fear and shame around now feeling in the closet not only about my sexual orientation and gender presentation, but also feeling in the closet about being formerly incarcerated. I swore that "normal" people could tell where I had just been. Once I had taken all the online classes possible, I had to make a choice between not going to school anymore (since I would have to attend in person) or trying it out. When I decided I did want to try taking classes in person, I searched the Laney College course catalog for classes and came upon a class called "Woman of Color" taught by instructor Alicia Caballero-Christenson. I refer to Alicia lovingly as my *profe* (prɔ-fê), which is a term of endearment, short for the Spanish word for professor. I decided to try the class and as soon as I heard my *profe* use terms like matrix of oppression, mass incarceration, queerphobic, transphobic, patriarchy, and intersectionality, so much began to make sense. I began to realize that I had been pathologized and oppressed, and this was by design, not by coincidence. The classroom experience Alicia co-created with students affirmed and connected my personal experiences. I knew then that she was someone that I could talk to candidly and that she holistically accepted me not despite, but precisely because of who I am and what I have experienced. Moreover, thanks to Alicia, I considered Laney College a place where I could belong and learn to live a positive life. Also, in my *profe's* class, I learned about women that had unapologetically claimed their power and took bold steps to be at the forefront of true justice and liberation; women like Dolores Huerta, Audre Lorde, and Gloria Anzaldua. In Profe Alicia's class, for the first time, I was able to give shape to abstract shackles that had taken away my ability to wander forward toward my authentic essential self and any opportunity of ever thriving—let alone of someday achieving self-love and self-actualization.

At my community college, I found a meaningful employment opportunity at a brand new campus-based program, Restoring Our Communities (ROC), that supports formerly incarcerated students. This program came to my attention, through my *profe*, as I was about to transfer. Thanks to ROC's director and ethnic studies instructor, Roger Viet Chung, my incarceration history, my sexual orientation, and gender presentation were affirmed and honored; I was an asset to ROC not despite these factors, but precisely because of them. For me, the path through college was made possible by finding people that wanted to hear me out, who shared their knowledge, and supported me as I became my best self, family member, friend, loved one, and community member. I want to dedicate my narrative to Alicia and Roger, without whom my life would not be full of love, authenticity, and courage.

CONSIDERING A STUDENT VOICE: "DOING BETTER: HOLDING COLLEGES ACCOUNTABLE" BY CADENCE DOBIAS

If a transvestite doesn't say I'm gay and I'm proud and I'm a transvestite, then nobody else is going to hop up there and say I'm gay and I'm proud and I'm a transvestite for them.
—Marsha P. Johnson

I entered community college at 17 years old. Following a traumatic brain injury and a move from Monterey, California to San Diego, California for medical treatment, I decided to attend community college as a means to recover and prepare for my future. My community college experience was undeniably positive. I was able to complete my traumatic brain injury recovery programs, get an early diagnosis for a heart condition, and become greatly involved in student leadership and political advocacy. However, this positive experience was not without its ups and downs. As a disabled biracial queer girl trying to figure out community college, I was a disgrace to my family and a walking sign that seemed to say "unprepared, underrepresented, and tired."

My community college experience greatly shaped not only my identity but also how I chose to present myself as a result of my interactions at the college. Coming from an incredibly conservative home, I went into community college very ashamed of who I was. Being disabled was already a private shame I held, but being queer too? That was something I didn't dare bring up to those around me, my friends, or even at times myself. Things changed when I registered for my first theater class at Grossmont Community College. I lacked confidence and communication skills, but that didn't stop me from registering once my counselor said it would look good on my transfer applications. Little did I know I would be walking into a class where the real material I would be learning would be about myself—things I would take with me for a lifetime.

The professor opened the class by explaining that it would always be a safe space, that he would always be here for us as people and as students and proceeded to list resources for us from food insecurity resources to LGBT safe spaces. This would not be the only time he did this as he either began or ended his class in a similar fashion for the rest of the semester. What he didn't know is that this was the first time I was in a class where a professor had ever done that. Over the duration of the semester, he shifted away from the base of the material to encourage us to view it more as an analysis of ourselves—our biases, our beliefs, what we needed to improve, and how we could push ourselves to be better people.

Yet, it all led up to the day in which he and I had a long discussion about queer safety in community college. The following week we offered a survey to every student in that class so they could express their pronouns and chosen name. He later told me that he then began offering that at the beginning of all of the classes he taught.

As I became more open, he began asking more about my identity. What struggles had I experienced as specifically concerning my sexuality and with my disability? How have these made me change to adapt to my surroundings?

It was questions such as these that began to push me towards being more expressive with my identity. Over the course of that semester, I began to come out of my shell more and more. By the next semester I was out to all of my friends and coworkers. I also came out to myself. I stopped denying my identity and being ashamed of who I was. I looked my own parents in the eyes to explain that although I love them, I had to be honest with them about my sexual identity to begin to love myself. I became the person I wanted to be, but I was so terrified to acknowledge that part of me. This process has not been without struggles.

My community college campus frequently allowed protestors and booths to parade around the school with signs that said, "All Gays Go to Hell"; "We Can Help Fix You"; or "It Isn't Natural." These words were shown right in front of my face as I tried to go to class. I would scrub my hands in the bathroom trying to wash away any semblance of this blatant homophobia presented in front of me. This greatly took away from my educational experience and that of my peers as well. A space that was supposed to be a positive and safe area for us was instead a display of blatant homophobia. Yet, this issue was not specific to our college. Whatever community college we went to we saw the same issues. Lack of representation, few resources, protestors walking around the campus—some going from classroom to classroom. When colleges didn't do anything, it showed that no community college was an active ally. Later, community colleges in the area started to release statements or present some form of rainbow merchandise. However, it was rare that they also followed up to provide resources, support programs, or take an active step to be an ally on campus. A rainbow flag might be displayed, but under it were people saying that being LGBTQ+ was a choice, a choice that would end with eternal damnation.

It was difficult to study for upcoming exams while being blasted with these various forms of hate. Additionally, the programs instituted within my community college and those of my friends were underdeveloped, underprepared for the influx of students each semester, and often lacked the representation needed to provide a safe space for students. It seemed as though these community colleges had the right thought. They wanted to support us students. They wanted to be allies. Yet, it was misplaced as they put more thought into their words than actually attempting to create a safe learning environment for students. These colleges did not acknowledge the disproportionate number of LGBTQ+ community college students who experience food and housing insecurity. City resources were not prepared to assist these students with their needs. There were many positive ideas, but little impactful follow through.

This led to many discussions between myself and my peers on what we wished they could have done or what would've improved these things.

One consistent theme was that to improve, community colleges must shift their perspective from *wanting* to be an ally to choosing to be one.

Community colleges that want to be an ally often make meaningless statements and attempt programs which are not prepared to genuinely assist students. Community colleges with an active ally mindset are able to recognize that to maintain a positive learning environment, they must prioritize marginalized students and choose to take action—whether that be with action to have safer class environments, LGBTQ programs, resources, and funding allocation.

There has to be a shift from just thinking about the needs of diverse students, to fundamentally shifting to where nothing is done without the consideration and voice of diverse students' needs. I saw what this shift and practice looked like when I attended that theater class. He didn't need to prioritize these things because he built it into the structure of his classes. He knew the needs of his students and he chose to address them at the core of his courses so that he could put the students above all else. Beyond that class, I did not receive the support I needed.

There was never a time outside of that class where my identity was affirmed, where I felt that there were safe spaces or resources that were openly provided to me. I believe that these issues within community colleges extend beyond its queer communities and into its other underserved groups. There are few and far between resources for other groups, such as veterans, biracial students, international students, or DACA students. There are often statements made on behalf of the college, but when you look deeper you cannot see it in action. The fundamental change necessary to genuinely support students—queer and the marginalized students—is to turn from a conversational ally to an active ally in all aspects.

CONSIDERING A STUDENT VOICE. *MY CLOSET'S EMBELLISHMENTS* BY ASH TANDOC (THEY/THEM)

I am transgender, and this doesn't mean that I am unlovable.
—Lana Wachowski (2012)

As most closets do, mine lives in my room.
I leave it behind when I go out.

My closet's a room in itself;
it's embellished with hints of myself—

a color scheme here, a flower over there
just barely peeking out from the cracks.

My closet is a vast room in itself;
it's full of pride, rage, lust—

all the sins that haunt me
that I have painted into virtues;

it's full of blushing dreams
and purple-tinged schemes

that tell me my future, like tarot cards
divining a poor sinner's luck.

But, like any future, it's a wavering
portrait of watercolor, beautiful and tenuous—

so the dreams stay in the closet,
its hopes are small, but burning, points of light.

My favorite thing to do is leave the closet in my room
after pick-pick-picking the best accessories to leave with

and venture into a world
of open wardrobes—

it's the loveliest thing to enter
a room so open like a garden

with people who understand what
it's like to have a closet of their own.

Some have splintered theirs,
some, like me, have theirs intact.

Whatever the case, we've all got our closets
and we've all got our ornaments.

I love them—the ones with the closets
and the ones with the fiercest compassions

(for compassion is a blazing fire
that comforts us and repels the oppressors).

> It is a terrible, dreadful tragedy
> when I have to leave them behind
>
> and confront my mirrored closet
> and its vast, vast room.
>
> Still, I know that my world
> of open wardrobes
>
> will be there when I venture again.

As community college educators, administrators, and researchers we are often called upon to make policies or create new knowledge to improve campus experiences for our queer and trans students. However, these decisions can often get made in the absence of input from the students who these policies most directly impact. The student stories presented above provide us with the rich details we often lack when called upon to reimagine our campuses or begin establishing services. The beauty of these stories is heartbreaking, uplifting, and certainly a call to action to create campuses that welcome and affirm our diverse and amazing students.

8

Conclusion

As we conclude this book, we want to leave you with a few other items that have more to do with you as a person. Social justice education and advocacy are critical to our world and to educational systems, but it is not easy to separate work from life and from one's identity. The following sections aim to provide some insight into how to sustain yourself, keep growing and learning, and where you might want to plan long term. The road to justice and liberation for LGBTQ+ people will take multiple lifetimes, and we need all of us to be healthy, whole, and sustained in this movement.

Identity and Tokenization as an LGBTQ+ Professional

If you are serving in the LGBTQ+ staff or faculty role at your college, it can take over all other of your other identities and even your professional role or background. Those who become vocal about a specific justice issue can quickly become seen as the radical or angry queer person. As professional educators, we do not want to be seen as single-issue people; however, this can be the case if no one else is willing to advocate for LGBTQ+ on a college campus. Faculty or staff members in LGBTQ+ roles are often seen as the expert on LGBTQ+ issues, but that is where their knowledge and skills stop. Any prior experience or other areas of expertise can get ignored or minimized. It can create challenges with long-term career opportunities and pigeonhole professionals. This being said, it is not to discourage LGBTQ+ professionals, but to be aware of perception and create strategies to avoid letting others limit their role or knowledge if it is a concern.

Serving in a public LGBTQ+ role can also lead to tokenization, especially if LGBTQ+ becomes enticing to the public, the board, or media. As colleges become more aware and interested in doing LGBTQ+ work, they often may turn to the few or only LGBTQ+ at the college. At times, the LGBTQ+ professional may not be willing to serve in this role due to limited time or emotional capacity. At one institution where I (Joshua) served in an LGBTQ+ role, I was quickly seen as having only one identity (queer, very queer). When colleagues would talk to me, even in social situations, they only talked to me about LGBTQ+ topics, such as this new gay movie they saw or that their gay cousin came out. It became exhausting and even annoying. People did not see me for my other identities, such as being multiracial or Asian American. In this role, other employees minimized all of my prior experience related to research and assessment or marketing and public relations. I was only asked to speak to LGBTQ+ issues, and I had to push to be seen as a well-rounded educator. Even after moving out of this role, I was still regularly asked to speak on behalf of LGBTQ+ people for the institution and lead committees. I valued the work and experience serving as an LGBTQ+ professional, but I had to be cognizant and strategic about my career development as well as protecting my emotional resources.

As an LGBTQ+ professional, I (Joshua) struggled to maintain my own emotional wellness on multiple occasions. I have experienced trauma, violence, and exclusion due to my sexual orientation and gender expression and healing is a lifetime journey. Most of the time I was able to separate my experience from my work enough to be effective and serve students. At times, the situation I was managing triggered past trauma, and I had to separate myself and ask a coworker to take over. In one situation, I was mediating a restorative justice circle where two feminine queer men had been assaulted because of their identities. My role was to facilitate and guide the group to name impact, restore community, and create an environment where people are safe, and others are held accountable. This situation was similar to an experience I previously had, and I struggled to be in that space. There were numerous other occasions where my trauma as a queer fem person made it difficult to show up in role and be effective. At times when I need space for my own healing, I was expected to show up as a resource for students. In order to be effective, I had to know my own triggers, traumas, and have strategies to serve students while also acknowledging what I needed as a person. In the end, my pain and experiences have aided me in being empathetic, trustworthy, and powerful as a change agent. The work for an LGBTQ+ professional is deeply personal, and it is nearly impossible to separate work from self.

Finding Resilience

The work of changing culture on campus and fighting for the rights of marginalized students is hard—but we can do hard! One thing to remember when doing this work is that you will lose more battles than you will win! That may be hard to hear, but it is absolutely imperative that you do not mark the success of your work by the number of times you are told "No," because to be frank, you will be told "No" a lot. We want to leave you with some strategies to make the work a little easier to navigate.

First, make yourself a campus resource. Cross collaboration with departments embeds your work across the institution and is your best bet for long-term systemic change; this is also a chance to develop a cadre of individuals who can also provide training, insight, and advocacy when you are not available. When there are few individuals on a campus doing queer and trans advocacy you may become the person "for all the queer stuff." This is to be avoided at all costs. When this work is viewed as the purview of one individual, then institutional change is unlikely. To develop this type of wide-ranging campus support you should try to present during trainings at the beginning of each semester, offer to come to classes to give lectures, and attend town halls or open meetings with executive staff and ask about plans to meet the needs of queer and trans students on campus. During these meetings with key decision makers, try to identify allies and accomplices and cultivate those relationships; this is another key strategy to navigating this work.

Most colleges are hierarchical in nature, so cultivating relationships with key decision makers is imperative to moving the needle towards a more equitable and just college. Those folks higher in the organization have more access to the workings of the system and finances. It is surprising how much work can be accomplished when people in seats of power are aware of and interested in your work. Remember that folks have to meet the needs of many people and are often juggling many competing demands. Make it easy for them to say "Yes" to you!

As mentioned above, this work can be draining so it is important that you also consider how you will manage the inevitable feelings of burnout.

As cliché as it might sound, remember to practice self-care. Find colleagues and friends who support you and can hold space for you when the demands become overwhelming.

It is important to find nuggets of hope and remember why we are fighting so hard. I (Emilie) often come back to an interaction I had early on in my tenure as the Pride Center coordinator. There were several of us on campus who had been pushing for a name policy that would allow students to indicate a lived name that was different from their legal name. This is hugely consequential to our transgender and gender non-conforming students. As the newly minted coordinator of our just established Pride Center, I decided this would be my fight. I took this issue to the district, emailing everyone I could conceivably find who I thought might be able to help, when they ignored my email—I sent another one. When they ignored those, I called. When they did not answer the phone, I showed up at their office. I asked around about who made decisions, learned about the IT structure, and the basic ways in which names were coded into our system. I tried to ingratiate myself with anyone I thought might be able to help me.

Fast forward many, many, many long bruising months, and the policy was enacted. I must admit that I felt beaten down by how hard it had been to get this change made and felt unsure about whether I had the emotional fortitude to go through that for each change that needed to be made. Soon after, the Pride Center was hosting a social event and a young person approached me. This young scholar spoke painfully and passionately about their transition, about how hard it has been for them at home and at school, and how unsure they were about continuing with school as they would have to ask professors to call them a different name and they feared being outed and harmed. I asked the student for 5 minutes of their time, I entered their live name in our services and assured them that no one other than financial aid would even know what their legal name was. The student sobbed. This change allowed this student to feel safer, to feel seen, and to want to keep going. Okay I thought, I can do this!

Remember that even though the wins may be small, especially at first, these accomplishments move the needle a little bit each time. Most importantly, remember that even seemingly small changes can have huge impacts on a student's life.

(Lemuel) As a cisgender gay male, I find that I have spoken up and out about oppression as an administrator. My access to funding has afforded me the ability to bring about change for LGBTQ+ individuals. As I reflect on my past as a dean of academic support and programs, I remember that one director of libraries at a small community college in a small Midwestern town wanted to make sure that our academic programs and academic center was a place where LGBTQ+ and others could find the resources they needed to survive and thrive. There was no LGBTQ+ center, but our director of libraries made sure she brought requests for a host of items for me to support. All of her requests made sense to me, her strategy for how she perceived her people, LGBTQ+ individuals, and their need for support was important. She wrote to faculty and spoke to classrooms about the resources of the library. She enlisted other LGBTQ+ individuals at the community college to also join her in the efforts to create a community where all could learn and belong. Her passion also spilled over into the community. She was able to be successful because I was supportive of her efforts and understood the impact her work (our work) would have throughout the greater community. As a dean of three different colleges of education, I have also intervened on the behalf LGBTQ+ candidates on job interviews to speak truth to situations that could have gone in the wrong direction. Having the courage to do what is right and to call others' behaviors of discrimination and bias to light has been important for me and to the faculty and staff I have supported. I have also been shunned by individuals, it does not matter gender, race, or sexuality, just because I refused to fit a stereotype or to be placed in a box, and this cuts across all of my identities. So, one learns to stand in the sun and beams the brightest that he can in order to light the way for others. It can be a lonely existence, to be Black, gay, mixed race marriage, southern, Christian, and an administrator in the academy. I find that I am never enough of anything or too much of something else. However, thank God I have enough individuals who are the right individuals to love me and to support me when needed. One does not need the world to love them, just enough friends who will. We should never forget the words of a tweet from the late Honorable John Lewis, "Do not get lost in a sea of despair. Be hopeful, be optimistic. Our struggle is not the struggle of a day, a week, a month, or a year, it is the struggle of a lifetime. Never, ever be afraid to make some noise and get in good trouble, necessary trouble" (Bote, 2020, para. 4).

The COVID 19 pandemic has changed life around the world, and for many it has been traumatic and dramatic. It has heightened awareness of the divides related to economic, health, gender, geographical, and racial disparities in all countries. Reflecting on the racism and discrimination happening around the world and in my own communities towards marginalized populations, we have been called into a consciousness that requires us to pause, acknowledge the inequities, and to act in ways to educate, build trust, and to hold each other accountable. Of course, we all get tired, of course the time is now. However, the key is in the "we"—we are all responsible for what happens in our society, communities, and homes, and we should speak out and speak up when there are inhuman activities that diminishes our progress. What I have learned as a member of the faculty and administration is to listen without judgment; to speak without venom, and to collaborate without preconceived notions. To practice having faith in my peers; being authentic, vulnerable, and courageous as a leader; and to "never, ever be afraid to make some noise and get in good trouble, necessary trouble" for the rights of those who have been oppressed, who are too tired to carry on, and who have lost their voices in the fight for justice.

National Resources

We hope this book has been a useful resource to guide your college towards better serving LGBTQ+ students. We know this process takes years and even decades. We hope to make sure you can connect to national organizations that continue to provide resources, community, and spaces to get support and promising practices. Here are several organizations:

1. *Consortium of Higher Education LGBT Resource Professionals*: The organization has a vision to create higher education environments where LGBTQ+ people, inclusive of all of intersecting identities, are fully liberated. They support individuals who work on campuses to educate and support people of diverse sexual orientations and gender identities, as well as advocate for more inclusive policies and practices through an intersectional and racial justice framework.
2. *National LGBTQ Task Force*: The organization advances full freedom, justice, and equality for LGBTQ+ people. They are building a future where everyone can be free to be their entire selves in every aspect of their lives.
3. *NASPA (Student Affairs in Higher Education) Gender and Sexuality Knowledge Community*: The NASPA Gender and Sexuality Knowledge Community provides avenues for both social and professional involvement. Their goal is to encourage personal and professional growth, increased awareness and acceptance of professionals and students, and to promote understanding of gender and sexuality needs.
4. *ACPA (College Student Educators International) Coalition for Sexuality and Gender Identities:* The coalition is charged to increase awareness, eliminate oppression, and provide support for the LGBTQ+ com-

munity in higher education, for faculty, students, and staff. They strive to further professional competencies related to topics such as campus climate, equity, identity development, research and scholarship, and program development for the LGBTQ+ community.

Further Research and Practice

There are several areas within the community college system that are beyond the scope of this book but need attention to create more equitable colleges. First, it is important to understand that the queer and trans student population live and study in the shadows of their campuses. Few community college districts survey students regarding their sexual orientation and gender identity, consequently, queer and trans students are not recognized in the demographic profiles of our student population and as a direct result are often overlooked in institutional planning. This lack of data is a glaring problem in the attempts to extend campus equity work to LGBTQ+ students. In addition to lack of data on LGBTQ+ students, there is also a dearth of research on students' experiences on our campuses. In order to provide services for students, we must ask them what they need. While this assertion seems basic, it requires a substantial investment of time and advocacy. It is important to conduct quantitative and qualitative studies on campus climate for LGBTQ+ students on campus. We must use this data to inform our programming on campus and help our administrators understand the campus climate for queer and trans students.

In addition to data and research, we must center the voices of our most marginalized students. Research clearly indicates that while queer individuals still face discrimination, harassment, and violence, these affronts are more likely to be borne by the trans community and particularly by transgender and gender non-conforming individuals of color. Trans gender and gender non-conforming individuals face deplorable levels of violence and harassment for their identity. We must acknowledge that oppression lives at the intersections of students marginalized identities. For far too long, the fight for LGBTQ+ liberation has been "whitewashed" focusing on the experiences of White people. It is imperative that we focus on the fight for racial liberation with a focus on the voices of our BIPOC (Black, indigenous, and people of color) queer and trans students.

Finally, it is important that we also need to work on the recruitment and retention of LGBTQ+ professionals. It is important that we consider how we begin outreach to our queer and trans colleagues to encourage them to apply to our institutions and to work to make our campus environments conducive to queer and trans employees to live openly and authentically. A part of challenging policies and procedures that exclude or marginalize queer and trans students is to also interrogate policies around hiring as well as the ways in which our LGBTQ+ colleagues experience the campus environment.

References

11 Facts LGBT Life in America. (n.d.). DoSomething.org. https://www.dosomething.org/us/facts/11-facts-lgbt-life-america

Adams v. School Board of St. Johns County, No. 18-13592 (11th Cir. 2020). https://law.justia.com/cases/federal/appellate-courts/ca11/18-13592/18-13592-2020-08-07.html

Ahmed, S. (2006a). *Queer phenomenology: Orientations, objects, others.* Duke University Press.

Ahmed, S. (2006b). Orientations: Toward a queer phenomenology. *GLQ: A Journal of Lesbian and Gay Studies, 12*(4), 543–574.

American Association of Community Colleges. (n.d.). *Community college enrollment crisis? Historical trends in community college enrollment.* https://www.aacc.nche.edu/wp-content/uploads/2019/08/Crisis-in-Enrollment-2019.pdf

American School Counselor Association. (2012). *The ASCA national model: A framework for school counseling program* (3rd ed.).

Astin, A. (1984). Student involvement: A development theory for higher education. *Journal of College Student Development, 40,* 518–529.

Baams L. (2018). Disparities for LGBTQ and gender nonconforming adolescents. *Pediatrics, 141*(5), 1–10.

Baams, L., Wilson, B. D. M., & Russell, S. T. (2019). LGBTQ youth in unstable housing and foster care. *Pediatrics, 143*(3), 1–11.

Badgett, M. V. L., Choi, S. K., & Wilson, B. D. M. (2019, October). *LGBT poverty in the United States: A study of differences between sexual orientation and gender identity groups.* The Williams Institute.

Bailey, T., Jaggars, S. S., & Jenkins, D. (2015). *Redesigning Americas community colleges: A clearer path to student success.* Harvard University Press.

Baker, J. A. (1991). Gay nineties: Addressing the needs of homosexual community and junior college students and faculty. *Community/Junior College Quarterly of Research and Practice, 15*(1), 25–32.

Bandyopadhyay, M. (2016, October 22). *Be yourself, the world will adjust* [Video]. YouTube. https://www.youtube.com/watch?v=Hmw6sUmm0mU

Barnett, B. G., Hall, G. E., Berg, J. H., & Camarena, M. M. (1999). A typology of partnerships for promoting innovation. *Journal of School Leadership, 9*, 484–510.

Beck, A. J., Cantor, D., Hartge, J., & Smith, T. (2013, June). *Sexual victimization in juvenile facilities reported by youth, 2012: National survey of youth in custody, 2012* (NCJ 241708). U.S. Department of Justice Office of Justice Programs Bureau of Justice Statistics. https://www.bjs.gov/content/pub/pdf/svjfry12.pdf

Beemyn, B. (2003). The silence is broken: A history of the first lesbian, gay, and bisexual college student groups. *Journal of the History of Sexuality, 12*(2), 205–223. https://doi.org/10.1353/sex.2003.0075

Bhattar, R. G. (2019). *"We exist!": Sense of belonging for Indian international LGBQ students in U.S. higher education* [Doctoral dissertation, University of California–Los Angeles]. https://escholarship.org/uc/item/015884cn

Bostock v. Clayton County, Board of Commissioners, 140 S. Ct. 1731 (2020). https://www.supremecourt.gov/opinions/19pdf/17-1618_hfci.pdf

Bote, J. (2020, July 18). 'Get in good trouble, necessary trouble': Rep. John Lewis in his own words. *USA Today.* https://www.usatoday.com/story/news/politics/2020/07/18/rep-john-lewis-most-memorable-quotes-get-good-trouble/5464148002/

Bowleg, L. (2008). When Black+ lesbian+ woman≠ Black lesbian woman: The methodological challenges of qualitative and quantitative intersectionality research. *Sex Roles, 59*(5–6), 312–325.

Bracken, W., & Wood, J. L. (2019). Examining the mirror effect: Culturally relevant images in a testing environment. *Western Journal of Black Studies, 43*(1–2), 1–8.

Bronski, M. (2011). *A queer history of the United States.* Beacon Press.

Brown, D. (2019, June 28). Marsha P. Johnson: Transgender hero of Stonewall riots finally gets her due. *USA Today.* https://www.usatoday.com/story/news/investigations/2019/03/27/black-history-marsha-johnson-and-stonewall-riots/2353538002/

Brown. G. R., & Jones, K. T. (2015). Health correlates of criminal justice involvement in 4,793 transgender veterans. *LGBT Health, 2*(4), 1–9.

Bryan, J., & Henry, L. (2008). Strengths-based partnerships: A school–family–community partnership approach to empowering students. *Professional School Counseling, 12*(2), 149–156. https://doi.org/10.1177/2156759X0801200202

Bryan, J., & Henry, L. (2012). A model for building school–family–community partnerships: Principles and process. *Journal of Counseling & Development, 90*(4), 408–420. https://doi.org/10.1002/j.1556-6676.2012.00052.x

Bukoski, B. E., & Hatch, D. K. (2015). "We're still here...we're not giving up": Black and Latino men's narratives of transition to community college. *Community College Review, 44*(2), 99–118. https://doi.org/10.1177/0091552115621385

Burgess, C. (1999). Internal and external stress factors associated with the identify development of transgendered youth. *Journal of Gay & Lesbian Social Services, 10*(3/4), 35–47.

Community Colleges; California College Promise, A.B. 19 (2017). https://home.cccapply.org/en/money/california-college-promise-grant

California Courts. (2022, May 22). *Proposition 8 cases*. https://www.courts.ca.gov/6464.htm

Cass, V. C. (1984). Homosexual identity formation: Testing a theoretical model. *Journal of Sex Research, 20*(2), 143–167.

Castro, E. L., Hunter, R. K., Hardison, T., & Johnson-Ojeda, V. (2018). The landscape of postsecondary education in prison and the influence of Second Chance Pell: An analysis of transferability, credit-bearing status, and accreditation. *The Prison Journal, 98*(4), 405–426. https://doi.org/10.1177/0032885518776376

Chen, G. (2020, March 9). LGBT studies major: A first for community colleges. *Community College Review*. https://www.communitycollegereview.com/blog/lgbt-studies-major-a-first-for-community-colleges

Choi, S. K., Wilson, B. D. M., Shelton, J., & Gates, G. (2015). *Serving our youth 2015: The needs and experiences of lesbian, gay, bisexual, transgender, and questioning youth experiencing homelessness*. The Williams Institute With True Colors Fund.

Consortium of Higher Education LGBT Resource Professionals. (n.d.) *Find an LGBT Center*. https://www.lgbtcampus.org/find-an-lgbtq-campus-center

Couloute, L., & Kopf, D. (2018, July). *Out of prison & out of work: Unemployment among formerly incarcerated people*. Prison Policy Initiative. https://www.prisonpolicy.org/reports/outofwork.html

Cox, L. (2016, January 10). *Golden Globe Awards speech*. Los Angeles, CA.

Crenshaw, K. (1989). Demarginalizing the intersection of race and sex: A Black feminist critique of antidiscrimination doctrine, feminist theory, and antiracist politics. *University of Chicago Legal Forum, 1*(8), 139–167.

Crenshaw, K. (1991). Mapping the margins: Intersectionality, identity politics, and violence against women of color. *Stanford Law Review, 43*(6), 1241–1299.

D'Augelli, A. R. (1991). Gay men in college: Identity processes and adaptations. *Journal of College Student Development, 32*(2), 140–146.

Diversity Best Practices. (2018, March 6). https://www.diversityincbestpractices.com/topic/employee-resource-groups

Duran, A. (2019). A photovoice phenomenological study exploring campus belonging for queer students of color. *Journal of Student Affairs Research and Practice, 56*(2), 153–167.

Ellis, S. J. (2009). Diversity and inclusivity at the university: A survey of the experiences of lesbian, gay, bisexual, and trans (LGBT) students in the UK. *Higher Education, 57*(6), 723–739. http://shura.shu.ac.uk/117/1/fulltext.pdf

Emerson, J., & Bassett, L. (2008). *Supporting success: Improving higher education outcomes for students from foster care.* Casey Family Programs. https://www.casey.org/media/SupportingSuccess.pdf

Epstein, J., & Van Voorhis, F. (2010). School counselors' roles in developing partnerships with families and communities for student success. *Professional School Counseling, 14*(1), 1–14.

Fassinger, R. E. (1991). The hidden minority: Issues and challenges in working with lesbian women and gay men. *The Counseling Psychologist, 19*(2), 157–176.

Feinberg, L. (1992). *Transgender liberation: A movement whose time has come.* World View Forum.

Flaskerud, J. H. (Ed.). (1999). Preface. Emerging nursing care of vulnerable populations. In *Nursing Clinics of North America, 34*(2).

Franklin, K. (1998, August 14–18). *Psychosocial motivations of hate crimes perpetrators: Implications for educational intervention* [Paper Presentation]. 106th Annual Convention of the American Psychological Association 1998, San Francisco, CA, United States.

Friedman, M. S., Marshal, M. P., Guadamuz, T. E., Wei, C., Wong, C. F., Saewyc, E. M., & Stall, R. (2011). A meta-analysis of disparities in childhood sexual abuse, parental physical abuse, and peer victimization among sexual minority and sexual nonminority individuals. *American Journal of Public Health, 101*(8), 1481–1494.

Gagnè, P., & Tewksbury, R. (1996). *Hide in plain sight: Conformist pressures and the transgender community.* Paper presented at the annual meetings of the Society for the Study of Social Problems, New York, NY.

Garvey, J. C., & Rankin, S. R. (2015). The influence of campus experiences on the level of outness among trans-spectrum and queer-spectrum students. *Journal of Homosexuality, 62*, 374–393. https://doi.org/10.1080/00918369.2014.977113

Garvey, J. C., Taylor, J. L., & Rankin, S. (2015). An examination of campus climate for LGBTQ community college students. *Community College Journal of Research and Practice, 39*(6), 527–541.

Gillborn, D. (2015). Intersectionality, critical race theory, and the primacy of racism: Race, class, gender, and disability in education. *Qualitative Inquiry, 21*(3), 277–287.

Goldrick-Rab, S., Baker-Smith, C., Coca, V., Looker, E., & Williams, T. (2019, April). *College and university basic needs insecurity: A national #RealCollege survey report.* https://hope4college.com/wp-content/uploads/2019/04/HOPE_realcollege_National_report_digital.pdf

González, Á., & Cataño, Y. (2020). Queering community college HSIs: An environmental scan of current programs and services for Latinx students. *Journal of Applied Research in the Community College, 27*(1), 81–95.

Gortmaker, V. J., & Brown, R. D. (2006). Out of the college closet: Differences in perceptions and experiences among out and closeted lesbian and gay students. *College Student Journal, 40*(3), 606–620.

Grant, J. M., Mottet, L. A., Tanis, J., Harrison, J., Herman, J. L., & Keisling, M. (2011). *Injustice at every turn: A report of the National Transgender Discrimination Survey*. National Center for Transgender Equality and National Gay and Lesbian Task Force.

Great Expectations: Fostering Powerful Change. (n.d.). Virginia Foundation for Community College Education. https://vfcce.org/wp-content/uploads/2021/08/GE_One-Sheet_MGC-digital-version.pdf

Grossman, A. H., & D'augelli, A. R., (2006). Transgender youth: Invisible and vulnerable. *Journal of Homosexuality, 51*(1), 111–123. https://doi.org/10.1300/J082v51n01_06

Gutiérrez, R. A. (1991). *When Jesus came the corn mothers went away: Marriage, sexuality, and power in New Mexico, 1500–1846*. Stanford University Press.

Harper, S. R. (2012). Race without racism: How higher education researchers minimize racist institutional norms. *The Review of Higher Education, 36*(1), 9–29.

Hillman, N., & Weichman, T. (2016). *Education deserts: The continued significance of "place" in the twenty-first century*. Viewpoints: Voices from the Field. American Council on Education.

Hurtado, A. (1999). *Intimate frontiers: Sex, gender, and culture in old California*. University of New Mexico Press.

Hurtado, S. (1994). The institutional climate for talented Latino students. *Research in Higher Education, 35*(1), 21–41.

In the Beginning. (n.d.). 2 Spirits. http://www.2spirits.com/PDFolder/about%20us.pdf

Irvine, A., & Canfield, A. (2016). The overrepresentation of lesbian, gay, bisexual, questioning, gender nonconforming and transgender youth within the child welfare to juvenile justice crossover population. *Journal of Gender, Social Policy, and Law, 24*(2), 243–261. https://doi.org/https://digitalcommons.wcl.american.edu/cgi/viewcontent.cgi?article=1679&context=jgspl

Ivory, B. T. (2012). Little known, much needed: Addressing the cocurricular needs of LGBTQ students. *Community College Journal of Research and Practice, 36*(7), 482–493.

James, S. E., Herman, J. L., Rankin, S., Keisling, M., Mottet, L., & Anafi, M. (2016). *The report of the 2015 U.S. Transgender Survey*. National Center for Transgender Equality.

Johns, S., Kilpatrick, S., & Whelan, J. (2007, August). Our health in our hands: Building effective community partnerships for rural health service provision. *Rural Society, 17*(1), 50–65.

Johnson, J. M. (2012). *Beyond surviving: From religious oppression to queer activism*. Purple Book Publishing.

Johnson, J. M., & Javier, G. (Ed.). (2017). *Queer people of color in higher education*. Information Age Publishing.

Kann, L., McManus, T., Harris, W. A., Shanklin, S. L., Flint, K. H., Queen, B., Lowry, R., Chyen, D., Whittle, L., Thornton, J., Lim, C., Bradford, D., Yamakawa, Y., Leon, M., Brener, N., & Ethier, K. A. (2018, June 15). Youth risk behavior surveillance—United States, 2017. *Morbidity and Mortality Weekly Report Surveillance Summaries, 67*(8), 1–114. http://dx.doi.org/10.15585/mmwr.ss6708a1

Keels, M. (2019). *Campus counter spaces: Black and Latinx for community at historically White universities.* Cornell University Press.

Lasker, R., Weiss, E., & Miller, R. (2001). Partnership synergy: A practical framework for studying and strengthening the collaborative advantage. *The Millbank Quarterly, 79*(2) 179–205.

Lawrence v. Texas, 539 U.S. 558 (2003). https://supreme.justia.com/cases/federal/us/539/558/

Leider, S. J. (2012). LGBTQ people on community college campuses: A 20-year review. *Community College Journal of Research and Practice, 36*(7), 471–474. https://doi.org/10.1080/10668926.2012.664084

Ma, J., & Baum, S. (2016). *Trends in community colleges: Enrollment, prices, student debt, and completion* [Research brief]. College Board Research. https://research.collegeboard.org/pdf/trends-community-colleges-research-brief.pdf

Mallon, G. P. (1999). A call for organizational trans-formation. *Journal of Gay and Lesbian Social Services, 10*(3/4), 131–142.

Martinez, E. F., & Munsch, P. (2019). Developing a sense of belonging in community college students. *About Campus: Enriching the Student Learning Experience, 24*(5), 30–34. https://doi.org/10.1177/1086482219896044

Meyer, I. H., Flores, A. R., Stemple, L., Romero, A. P., Wilson, B. D. M., & Herman, J. L. (2017). Incarceration rates and traits of sexual minorities in the United States: National inmate survey, 2011–2012. *American Journal of Public Health, 107*(2), 234–240.

Miranda, D. A (2010). Extermination of the *Joyas*: Gendercide in Spanish California. *GLQ: A Journal of Lesbian and Gay Studies, 16*(1–2), 253–284. muse.jhu.edu/article/372454

Moustakas, C. (1994). *Phenomenological research methods.* SAGE Publications.

National Center for Educational Statistics. (2021). *The condition of education 2020.* National Center for Educational Statistics. https://nces.ed.gov/programs/coe/indicator_csb.asp

Newport, F. (2018, May 22). *In U.S., estimate of LGBT population rises to 4.5%.* https://news.gallup.com/poll/234863/estimate-lgbt-population-rises.aspx

Nicolazzo, Z. (2017). *Trans* in college: Transgender students' strategies for navigating campus life and the institutional politics of inclusion.* Stylus Publishing.

Pascarella, E. T., & Terenzini, P. T. (2005). *How college affects students: A third decade of research* (Vol. 2). Jossey-Bass.

Preston, M. J., & Hoffman, G. D. (2015). Traditionally heterogendered institutions: Discourses surrounding LGBTQ college students. *Journal of LGBT Youth, 12*(1), 64–86.

Pusch, R. S. (2005). Objects of curiosity: Transgender college students' perceptions of the reaction of others. *Journal of Gay & Lesbian Issues in Education, 3*(1), 45–61, https://doi.org/10.1300/J367v03n01_06

Rankin, S. R. (2005). Campus climates for sexual minorities. *New Directions for Student Services, 2005*(111), 17–23. https://doi.org/10.1002/ss.170

Rankin, S., Weber, G., Blumenfeld, W., & Frazer, S. (2010). *2010 state of higher education for lesbian, gay, bisexual, and transgender people.* Campus Pride.

Rendon, L. I. (1994). Validating culturally diverse students: Toward a new model of learning and student development. *Innovative Higher Education, 19*(1), 33–51.

Renn, K. A. (2010). LGBT and queer research in higher education: The state and status of the field. *Educational Researcher, 39*(2), 132–141.

Renn, K. A., & Patton, L. (2010). *Campus ecology and environments.* In J. D. Schuh, S. R. Jones, & S. L. Harper (Eds.), Student services: A handbook for the profession (5th ed., pp. 242–256). Jossey-Bass.

Rider, N. G., McMorris, B. J., Gower, A. L., Coleman, E., & Eisenberg, M. E. (2018). Health and care utilization of transgender and gender nonconforming youth: A population-based study. *Pediatrics, 141*(3). https://doi.org/10.1542/peds.2017-1683

Riemer, M., & Brown, L. (2019). *We are everywhere: Protest, power, and pride in the history of queer liberation.* Ten Speed Press.

Ritchie, A. J., & Whitlock, K. (2018). Criminalization and Legalization. In D. Romesburg (Ed.), *The Routledge history of queer America* (pp. 300–314). Routledge.

Robinson, G. D. (2019). *Promoting persistence among LGBTQ community college students* [Doctoral dissertation, Illinois State University]. https://ir.library.illinoisstate.edu/etd/1041/?utm_source=ir.library.illinoisstate.edu%2Fetd%2F1041&utm_medium=PDF&utm_campaign=PDFCoverPages

Rocero, G. (2014, March 31). *Why I must come out* [Video]. YouTube. https://www.youtube.com/watch?v=mCZCok_u37w

Romer v. Evans, 517 U.S. 620 (1996). https://supreme.justia.com/cases/federal/us/517/620/

Ryan, C., & Futterman, D. (1997). Lesbian and gay youth: Care and counseling. *Adolescent Medicine, 8*(2), 207–374.

Sanlo, R. (1998). *Working with lesbian, gay, bisexual, and transgender college students: A handbook for faulty and administrators.* Greenwood Press.

Sanlo, R. L. (2004). Lesbian, gay, and bisexual college students: Risk, resiliency, and retention. *Journal of College Student Retention: Research, Theory and Practice, 6*(1), 97–110.

Sanlo, R. (2012). Guest editor. [Special issue]. *Community College Journal of Research and Practice, LGBT Issues in Community Colleges, 36*(7).

Sanlo, R. L., Rankin, S., & Schoenberg, R. (2002). *Our place on campus: Lesbian, gay, bisexual, transgender services and programs in higher education.* Greenwood Press.

Schlossberg, N. K., Lynch, A. Q., & Chickering, A. W. (1989). *Improving higher education environments for adults: Responsive programs and services from entry to departure.* Jossey-Bass.

Sears, C. (2015). *Arresting dress: Cross-dressing, law, and fascination in nineteenth-century San Francisco.* Duke University Press.

Strayhorn, T. L. (2012). Exploring the impact of Facebook and Myspace use on first-year students' sense of belonging and persistence decisions. *Journal of College Student Development, 53*(6), 783–796.

Strayhorn, T. L. (2012). *College students' sense of belonging: A key to educational success for all students.* Routledge.

Strayhorn, T. L. (2018). *College students' sense of belonging: A key to educational success for all students* (2nd ed.). Routledge.

Stryker, S. (2017). *Transgender history: The roots of today's revolution.* Da Capo Press.

Sylvia Rivera: Biography (1951–2002). (n.d.). Biography. https://www.biography.com/activist/sylvia-rivera

Tewksbury, R., & Gagne, P. (1996). Transgenderists: Products of non-normative intersections of sex, gender, and sexuality. *The Journal of Men's Studies, 5*(2), 105–129. https://journals.sagepub.com/doi/10.1177/106082659600500202

The Legacy Project. (n.d.). *Sylvia Rivera—Inductee: 1951–2002.* https://legacyprojectchicago.org/person/sylvia-rivera

The Public Safety and Rehabilitation Act of 2016 (the Act; Gen. Elec. [Nov. 8, 2016] Prop. 57)

Transgender Issues. (n.d.). Funders for LGBTQ Issues. https://lgbtfunders.org/resources/issues/transgender-issues

U.S. Department of Education, National Center for Education Statistics, Integrated Postsecondary Education Data System (IPEDS), 12-month Enrollment component 2018–19 provisional data.

Wachowski, L. (2012, October 20). *HRC Visibility Award acceptance speech.* https://www.hollywoodreporter.com/news/general-news/lana-wachowskis-hrc-visibility-award-382177/

Watson, L. W., & Johnson, J. M. (Eds.). (2013). *Authentic leadership: An engaged discussion of LGBTQ work as culturally relevant.* Information Age Publishing.

Wilson, B. D. M., Cooper, K., Kastanis, A., & Nezhad, S. (2014). *Sexual and gender minority youth in foster care: Assessing disproportionality and disparities in Los Angeles.* The Williams Institute, UCLA School of Law.

Wimberly, G. L. (2015). *LGBTQ issues in higher education: Advancing a research agenda.* American Educational Research Association.

Zamani-Gallaher, E. M., & Choudhuri, D. D. (2011). A primer on LGBTQ students at community colleges: Considerations for research and practice. *New Directions for Community Colleges, 2011*(155), 35–49.

About the Authors

Joshua Moon Johnson serves as the dean of student services and Title IX coordinator at American River College (community college) in Sacramento; he also previously served as the dean of equity programs and pathways at American River College. He has published three books. His first book, *Beyond Surviving: From Religious Oppression to Queer Activism* (2012, Purple Books Publishing) was a #1 best-seller on Amazon.com for gay and lesbian activism. Joshua's second book is a co-edited volume (with Lemuel W. Watson) about LGBTQ leaders in higher education, *Authentic Leadership: An Engaged Discussion of LGBTQ Work as Culturally Relevant* (2013, Information Age Publishing). Joshua's third book (co-edited with Gabriel Javier) is *Queer People of Color in Higher Education* (2017, Information Age Publishing). Joshua has also published numerous other book chapters and articles on topics related to diversity and social justice. Joshua previously served as the assistant dean/director of the Multicultural Student Center at UW–Madison and as the director of the LGBT Center at the University of California–Santa Barbara. Joshua received a doctorate in higher education and LGBT studies from Northern Illinois University, and a master's degree in student affairs from Binghamton University. Joshua also has a master's degree in marketing analysis from the University of Alabama and a bachelor's in business (marketing) from the University of South Alabama. Joshua is an alumnus of the Social Justice Training Institute and served as a cluster lead for the Student Social Justice Training Institute. Joshua has served as a faculty member at the University of Wisconsin–Madison,

Semester at Sea/University of Virginia, Concordia University–Portland, and Binghamton University–State University of New York. Joshua is a former chair of the NASPA (Student Affairs in Higher Education) MultiRacial Knowledge Community and held several positions with the Asian Pacific Islander Knowledge Community. Joshua is a board member for the Association of California Community College Administrators and serves as the equity team lead. He also serves as the vice president of the board for the Sacramento LGBT Community Center. Joshua has presented more than 40 national presentations and regularly serves as a trainer, consultant, and keynote speaker at campuses and conferences across the country.

Emilie Mitchell (she/her/hers) currently serves as the interim dean of social and behavioral sciences at Cosumnes River College. Previously she served as the American River College Pride Center faculty coordinator and the Los Rios Community College District, LGBTQ+ liaison. She also serves on advisory committees for the California Community College chancellor's office relating to LGBTQ+ students at the California Community Colleges and has served as the planner of the California Community College LGBTQ+ Summit for the last two years (2021 and 2022). In addition, Emilie served for almost a decade as a tenured faculty in psychology at American River College teaching Human Sexuality and Research Methods. Emilie earned a doctorate from the University of California–Davis in social psychology and a master's degree from California State University, Long Beach in general psychology with a focus on research design and analysis. She has presented at numerous professional conferences on serving the needs of LGBTQ students in the community college system as well as serving as a trainer and invited speaker to local and statewide groups.

Lemuel W. Watson is professor of leadership and change at Antioch Graduate School of Leadership and Change and provost professor of education, and senior scientist at the Kinsey Institute at Indiana University. As a certified mindfulness teacher by Search Inside Yourself Leadership Institute and as a certified mindfulness organizational strategist by the Institute for Organizational Science and Mindfulness, he currently focuses on mindful leadership and talent management to enhance work and learning environments. Watson is also a research fellow at the Center for Comparative & International Education at the Research Institute of Higher Education at Yunnan University. A seasoned leader whose career spans various industries, including educational, non-profit organizations, private, and entrepreneurship/small businesses. He has worked as a consultant on public policy and talent management issues worldwide. He has written books, monographs, and articles related to research on leadership, underrepresented populations,

LGBTQ+, public policy, and human development. He has been deeply engaged with the community as a personal and professional advocate through numerous arts, community, educational, and professional boards. He commits to leaving the world better than how he has found it. He has a genuine love for those he meets and is curious to get to know them authentically. His southern roots are deep and wide, yet he has a passionate love for the Midwest and other parts of the world that has helped shape his perspective on life. He moves about the world as an educator, advocate, leader, minister, poet, and collaborator with various individuals and groups. He believes there is no separating life into compartments but that each day and all experiences help one to become fully awake. Watson is also distinguished professor and dean emeritus and founding executive director of the Center for Innovation in Higher Education at the University of South Carolina and the former founding executive director of the Center for P–20 Engagement and dean of the College of Education at Northern Illinois University as well as former associate vice president, interim vice provost for diversity and inclusion, dean of the School of Education at Indiana University Bloomington. He is former host of Indiana University's podcast *On Illuminating: Truth and Light*, the South Carolina Educational Television series, *Carolina Classrooms*, and Fulbright scholar to Belarus.

www.ingramcontent.com/pod-product-compliance
Lightning Source LLC
Chambersburg PA
CBHW070625300426
44113CB00010B/1667